MW01180970

# WHY DO YOU HATE
# MONEY?

A FITNESS MARKETING GUIDE TO CREATE
CONTENT THAT KILLS, CRAFT COPY THAT
CONVERTS, AND MASTER THE SCIENCE
OF SELLING WITHOUT SELLING OUT

## JOEY PERCIA

For more information, please contact the Author at
joey@joeypercia.com

ISBN-13: 978-1-9812-3047-1

# An Incredible Free Gift Just For You!

What's going on!?

Before we get started, I wanted to say "Thank you" for investing in yourself and instilling your trust in me.

Your support means more than you realize.

The lessons you'll find in the coming pages are something I wish I were smacked in the face with ten years ago — it would have saved me tens of thousands of dollars, countless hours, and endless headaches.

But, sitting in the corner sulking isn't going to solve anything, so we're going to make the best of it.

It's no secret I believe copywriting, and marketing is one of the most important skills you can learn. Not only will it help you grow your business but the skills you develop during the process spill over into other areas of your life and will make you an indefensible member of any team.

Yes, this book will help you make more money, but it will also force you to become a better listener, communicator, leader, and person.

… That's a huge win for you and everyone in your life.

To speed up the process, I put together a few bonuses to make the process as quick, smooth, and painless as possible.

To claim your bonus goodies (worth $147) completely free, go to the link below:

www.WhyDoYouHateMoneyBook.com

The best way to help spread the love and help more people is by going to Amazon and leaving your honest review of the book if you find this book to be useful. This will help the book in front of more people.

Thank you for letting me be apart of your life. I appreciate you,

– Joey Percia


PS. Snap a picture of yourself with the book, post it up on social media, and email me a copy and I'll send you a free copy of the audiobook. Make sure you email me the picture at joey@joeypercia.com

## *Dedication*

This book is dedicated to my wife and #1 fan —
Lauren for your endless love

Dad, for everything —
putting your dreams on hold to support us

Mom, Matt, and Dina —
your support no matter what I do

# Contents

# Introduction

*"It's none of their business that you have to learn to write. Let them think you were born that way."*

— Ernest Hemingway

Right about now you're thinking "Why should I take the time to read this book?

…There's already truckloads of 6-figure business gurus telling me what I need to do, but I don't have the time or money to get done."

You have a valid point, and if I were you, I'd be asking myself the same question.

The truth is, there are countless books that you can get your hands on with a click of a few buttons to teach you the ins and outs of marketing and copywriting. Just look around.

So Why me? Why now? Why this book?

Those are honest questions, which I'll answer it shortly, but first I want you to picture the life-altering possibilities the lessons in this book can give you. I can say this with conviction because these experiences have changed my life and I continue to see them work for others who I'm fortunate enough have become clients of mine.

The truth is, your writing needs to communicate what you're selling and let people know your message is unique. You also need to do this in a way which persuades people to buy from you instead of your competitors. Otherwise; you'll get lost in the noise and bunched together with the rest of the other trainers, gyms, and countless health and fitness businesses.

There are lots of knowledgeable coaches who believe clients should flock to them because they're smart or they open a gym with fancy equipment.

Unfortunately, it doesn't work like that. The world doesn't owe you favors, and like many trainers, I learned these lessons the hard way.

You can be the greatest trainer in the world, but if you suck at marketing and communicating your message, you're going to get lost in the noise.

I can still remember working 16-18 hour days packed with personal training while trying to build my online fitness business. I was living in NYC at the time, and for a few months things were so rough, you could find me sleeping on a massage table packed away in the storage closet at the gym.

My thoughts were: I started a business, know a lot, spent thousands on certifications, business development, and a master's degree plus traveling the country to work for some of the best coaches – I deserve people's business!

But I didn't. It was foolish, childish, and wrong. I didn't understand it at the time, but the world doesn't work like that.

So, why should you read this book right now…?

**Because this is the book, I wish someone smacked me across the face with the day I decided I wanted to build a fitness business.**

Not because it's the most comprehensive, in-depth, complicated, and crazy copywriting and marketing book to ever bless this earth.

But, it's an easy and quick read that will teach health and fitness professionals everything they NEED to know about direct response marketing and copywriting… especially those who weren't blessed with the skill of writing (because I sure as hell wasn't.)

I had to learn direct response marketing and copywriting because I needed to stand out as an online coach. I wanted to make more money, have more time, and gain more freedom because I wanted to work from home. Nothing out of the ordinary.

I wanted more cash for vacation…To write in a way that moved people…To live comfortably in one of the most expensive cities in the world…To create content that people loved to read and would ultimately change their lives.

Today, I'm a full-time copywriter and direct marketing consultant for clients all over the world.

I work with businesses in dating, pharmacy, cannabis, habit-building, digital marketing, online business development, self-development, offline fitness for brick and mortar gyms, and of course, online fitness.

I write, coach, and consult with reputable coaches, brands, and companies I've looked up to for years.

Now, I use this book, a more in-depth online course, and other products and services to teach people just like you the skill of direct-response marketing so you can grow your business and brand without feeling like a sleazy salesman.

Health and fitness marketing can be complicated and confusing, but if there's a brain in that beautiful head of yours and you have the desire to be successful, you have what it takes to learn and apply this to your own business. And, I can show you how.

You will take the simple lessons you learn in this book and: establish authority, build trust, and use these authentic marketing secrets to create a successful career for yourself.

If you and I were sitting in front of each other chatting about life and business right now, I'm sure you'd say you like these skills because you'd like more money, right?

Maybe you want to use the money to travel, buy a new house, dump it into a kickass car, or piss it away on hookers and cocaine, that's up to you. No judgment.

My purpose of my book is to help you reach your dream goals.

I will give you the tools to take you from where you are right now to where you want to be. I will show you how to communicate, how to achieve goals for YOUR future customers and clients.

If you're already a world-class copywriter and marketer, this book isn't for you.

Here's who this book is for:

- Trainers who were told they don't need to learn how to market or sell themselves
- Coaches who hate selling and have a hard time selling themselves without feeling sleazy
- Gym owners who want to pack their gym, create a family environment and make an impactful change in their community
- Anyone who wants to learn how to use authenticity to persuade, influence, and get people to buy.
- Anyone who wants to help people while making more money and gaining freedom in their life.
- Anyone who is not a natural born writer (like myself) but wants to communicate with words that sell without

forking over 10's of thousands to hire a copywriter who doesn't care about your business.

The longer you wait to read this book, the more money, time, freedom, and happiness you're leaving behind.

… And shame on you if you have a gift for helping people but aren't doing everything in your power to let the world know about it.

Whether you're just starting your career, already have a successful business you want to scale and establish authority for, or just want to learn successful copywriting and marketing strategies to get more in business and life, this book will help you do that.

If you want to learn marketing secrets to write words that sell like a million-dollar copywriter (without actually being one), do NOT wait to read this book. It's time to take your fate into your own hands instead of handing it over to a self-proclaimed expert, marketing guru, or piss-poor business coach.

After you read this book, the ball will be in your court, and I hope you enjoy everything that comes along with the power in it.

– Joey Percia

**PS. The last thing I want to happen is for you to speed through this book just to check the box and say you read it without applying what's in here.**

Do NOT let this book find its way onto your bookshelf to collect dust while you buy 20 more books to soak up information without any action.

Instead, use these skills to help as many people as you can while building a business you love.

# But Why Do You Hate Money?

*"Writing isn't about making money, getting famous, getting dates, getting laid, or making friends. In the end, it's about enriching the lives of those who will read your work, and enriching your own life, as well."*

— Stephen King

… I know I did, or that's what it seemed like.

For as long as I can remember, I've had an unsettling relationship with money which pretty much controlled my life.

Not only did this crippling fear hold me hostage for the majority of my life, but it kept me from creating lasting memories and opportunities.

Like most people, this started when I was a kid. I grew up in a small town in Pennsylvania where there wasn't much money or opportunity. Small jobs, no hustle, nothing exciting happening.

We weren't poor growing up, but my family struggled with money. At the time, I didn't understand why because my dad worked his ass off and sacrificed so much to provide for us.

Anytime my parents had a disagreement I remember it relating to money. Without realizing it, I started doing the same in my life. I told myself I didn't need to make more money and downplayed the importance of making enough to live a life I enjoyed.

I followed the system and went to college and continued to my master's degree where one reoccurring theme played over and over again.

"You're not a salesman or a marketer… you're a scientist."

Unfortunately, knowing science didn't put food in my mouth and it sure as hell didn't pay for that piece of paper that cost me 40k+.

## Powerful (But Ethical) Influence and Persuasion Secrets… Operate With Care

It wasn't until I turned to "the dark side" and started to learn about copywriting and marketing that I realized money was just an exchange of value.

A few years back, I was living in Scottsdale, Arizona working as an assistant for a strength coach by the name of Bret Contreras. If you don't know Bret, he's been in the fitness industry for a long time and has built a massive following known as 'The Glute Guy.'

Bret has built his business without the use of hyped-up marketing claims and scummy sales techniques. Most consider him one of the 'anti-marketers.' If you pay close attention while you're reading this book, you'll notice the 'anti-marketing position' is a marketing strategy in itself (an extremely powerful one.)

Back when I was working with Bret, my girlfriend and I broke up. Homesick, heartbroken, and hopeless, I moved home to Pennsylvania with my tail between my legs. I was 26-years old and sleeping on my parent's couch with no job, hobbies, or purpose.

I had no idea what I wanted to do next, and it was a chore to drag myself off the couch every morning.

Naturally, I did the only thing I knew would dampen the pain. I partied my face off to fill the black hole in the pit of my stomach. At the time, I thought I figured out the perfect mixture of women, drugs, food, sex, alcohol, lying, and cheating to make the pain go away.

I got my hands on a book called "The Game — Penetrating The Secret Society of Pickup Artists" by Neil Strauss which introduced me to the underground world of pickup artists.

It turns out the pickup community wasn't for me, but Neil's book allowed me to find interests and develop skills I never thought about before: communication, influencing likability, captivating storytelling, charismatic personality traits, entertaining and engaging groups of people, and persuasion.

Which is funny to say when people ask me "Joey, how'd you get in copywriting?"

"Well... I took a bunch of skills I didn't know I had, mashed them together with new ones I learned from trying to pick up girls. I used Tinder, Bumble, and OkCupid to chat with women ages 24-35 within a 5-mile radius of Manhattan for amazing, engaging, and hilarious conversations for hours a day."

All of the sudden, conversations and sales become less awkward, scammy, and sleazy both in dating and coaching.

I didn't feel like I was selling out because I was finally able to show people how I could help them instead of talking to them in a way they didn't understand.

I fell in love with the entire process of copywriting and marketing which has given me a new career that has allowed me to work with amazing clients, travel the country to speak at events, and write the book you're reading right now.

What I was doing was valuable because it was changing people's lives.

It wasn't weird, spammy, or sleazy. I was truthful, real, and authentic and that's precisely what this book is all about.

Learning these skills are invaluable, will make you an indispensable member of any team and can be applied to any industry.

# A License To Print Money

Copywriting is a tool that gives you more choices, freedom, power, money, and control over everything in your life… so it's a pretty powerful tool.

You use persuasion throughout your entire life to get things you want…your job, spouse, your clients to build habits, even when pushing a group towards your favorite place to eat.

If you're not aware of what you're doing and how to do this — you're missing out on lots of money and positively changing the lives of lots of clients.

It's the one skill that allows you to increase sales in any business and decrease advertising costs at the same time. That means more money in your pocket or more money to put back into your business to scale even faster.

**Some call it a license to print money and others call it the most critical skill for every business owner and entrepreneur to have.**

The problem is, most sales copy uses old sleazy, scummy tactics that are way too 'over-the-top' for people like you and me… it just doesn't feel right.

That style may have worked back in the day, but it's overused and rapidly losing effectiveness, and that's not the reputation you want for you and your business.

Here's the good news, authentic marketing and copywriting

isn't a ridiculously hard skill to learn even if you're a terrible writer.

I'm living proof. In school, all my papers would get handed back to me with red marks, lines, and crosses plastered all over it.

## COPY CLIFF NOTES

The art and science of copywriting and marketing are based on influence, persuasion, and seduction… similar skills used by spies, scam artists, egomaniacs, and other evil human beings.

And while these skills can be used to manipulate, con, and trick people into buying low-quality offer, it's impossible to run a sustainable business that way.

At the same time, this equal skill can be used to save lives, help more people, provide a better life for you and your family, and protect others from the evil jerk offs mentioned above.

Words have a tremendous impact on how people feel, act, and react.

The marketing lessons in this book can be used for good or evil, but by reading this book, you're acknowledging you're the type of person who is going to use these skills in an authentic way that adds value to this world — not suck the life out of it.

# Copywriting and Marketing 101

*"Doing business without advertising is like winking at a girl in the dark. You know what you are doing, but nobody else does."*

— Stuart H. Britt

Before you go any further, I want to define common terms you'll find in this book.

## Direct Response Copywriting

The common mistake is to confuse copywriting with copyright. Copyright is the legal right to print, publish, perform, film, or record material, and let others do the same. It's the small print at the beginning of this book saying no one can rip off my work and claim it for their own.

Copywriting is a powerful tool used to communicate a message from one person to another and influence them to take action by appealing to their deep desires. This book focuses on direct response copywriting/marketing/advertising. These have a specific and measurable goal attached to them, such as a reply, like, share, buy, sign up, etc.

I will use the term copywriting and marketing interchangeably which will be referring to 'direct response marketing' not 'brand marketing,' which I will briefly explain.

## Brand Marketing

Also known as brand advertising and is NOT what this book is about. Brand marketing brings attention and awareness to a brand but doesn't create or ask for an action. Think of the TV commercials and most billboards that make up clever slogans, tag-lines, and jingles that generate no response. Brand marketing is useful for big companies with large marketing budgets, and again, not what this book is about.

## Products or Services

This is whatever you have to offer that is going to add value to your customer's life and help them solve a problem, reach a goal, etc. Products/Services could be a physical product (equipment or supplement), information product (book, course, ebook), service (1:1 training, seminar) or a combination of these. In some chapters, I will use the word product and others I will use word service depending on the lesson. Just know that I am referring to whatever you have that is going to help someone.

## Prospects

Can be people who have no idea who you are, don't realize they have a problem, know they have a problem but don't want to solve it, and the list goes on. Prospects are also commonly known as readers or leads. I don't like referring them to them as leads because it seems disingenuous. I will refer to anyone who is not a buyer or client, as a prospect or reader.

## Buyers

Simple. People who have trusted you and invested in what you have to offer. Buyers are commonly known as customers, clients, and even raving fans.

# Your Made-Up Stories Are Holding You Back From Being Successful

*"This is how you do it: You sit down at the keyboard and you put one word after another until it's done. It's that easy, and that hard."*

— Neil Gaiman

The stories we create in our minds are much scarier than reality.

The most significant barrier holding you back from getting what YOU want is your mind. I know because it happened to me for years and it's something I still struggle with today.

Do you know how long I've wanted to write a book but kept telling myself I would wait until **an arbitrary number, date, time, income**

It made no sense.

Adam Linkenauger, Co-founder of I Love Basketball and kickass marketer, has talked about how he's struggled to

ı his own mental barriers. As a national record
k and field athlete it was hard for him to remove
_ing his sole identify, and has mentioned this was
something that was hard to break through.

The first solution to breaking the shackles that hold you
hostage by your mind is to be aware of the situation and
understand that it's JUST in your mind. Luckily we just did
that.

The second step is to break free of it.

If you don't have a way to do this, you're bringing a butter
knife to a sword fight with a seasoned Samurai veteran. You
might as well quit now.

Every morning you wake up, you make a choice:

1) Listen to your bullshit stories about why you shouldn't,
   won't, can't, or don't want to do something because
   you aren't good enough

2) Do a few simple tasks that switch you from a reactive
   state where the stories your mind makes up controls
   you, to the attack where you control your life and don't
   fall victim to these stories.

This chapter is a quick breakdown of the common bullshit
stories you're telling yourself that will hold you back from
showing the world who you are and keeping you from
growing your business faster than ever.

# I'm Not A Good Writer

High Five! Neither am I.

As I said, I used to get papers back from my teachers covered in red ink, and I had to unlearn all the scientific writing I learned in undergrad and graduate school.

I remember Jordan Syatt and I looking back at our writing when we were in these college programs and laughing. We were trying to impress people with how much we knew, not how we could help them.

You don't have to be a "good" writer.

In fact, most copywriters and marketers are considered bad "writers, " but they're good salesman because they understand human psychology and string together words that get people to take action… which is what I will show you how to do.

They're good at speaking to an audience in a way that is understood, tell good stories, build trust, and have the reader take action.

## I Have To Be Funny, Clever, Cute, And Witty

The only thing worse than telling a joke and having no one laugh is doing the same thing in your writing.

It may seem better because you save yourself the in-person

embarrassment because you can't save the attempt. Your reader already left.

A good rule of thumb is: you should never have to explain a joke or it's no longer funny.

The goal is to be interesting and entertaining, not funny.

- **Funny:** no one goes to the class clown when they need help solving a problem.

- **Entertaining:** the guy at the party everyone loves to listen to and wants to be around. You go to this person when you need help.

Writing like this is called infotainment because it's valuable information that is entertaining to read.

Mark Bell of HowMuchYouBench.Net has built a wildly successful business by being the realest, goofiest, craziest version of himself. The same goes for powerlifting legend Donnie Thompson. I don't think either men would consider themselves business genius but they built successful businesses by helping people and being themselves.

The last thing you want to do is mimic someone else and come off like an impostor and push away an opportunity to work with great people.

# I Don't Want To Come Off Sleazy

Ok, don't.

The problem is, you see terrible marketing messages that are complete garbage stuffed with absurd claims that you know are never accurate.

*"LOSE 35 POUNDS in 5 WEEKS without exercise and this simple diet pill discovered by a 4-year-old child after being eaten by an Anaconda!!!!!!!!!!"*

Excuse me, while I swallow the throw-up in my mouth.

Not only do they reek like slimy, sleazy snake oil salesman, but everyone knows this is crap.

The good news is, extremely sleazy marketing messages aren't as fortunate today because the market has been accustomed to see thru them.

You should be understanding and empathetic to your customer. Let them know you care, their problems aren't all their fault, and some things in life just aren't in their control.

You want them to say "he gets me" not "who is this jackass trying to steal my hard-earned money."

# I Don't Have Anything New To Say

Sure you do.

"I don't have anything new to say" is one of the most common excuses for writer's block and not creating content that will grow your business and help tons of people.

I'm not going to go into writer's block here because I hulk smash it in another chapter, but I will say this… You don't have to revolutionize anything.

What you want to do is create a new opportunity or unique experience so your customer can differentiate you and what you have from the crap-filled market you're in. I say crap-filled market because every industry has it, some just have more than others, i.e., health and fitness.

Here, let me show you:

No one in this entire world has the same unique experiences, knowledge, lessons, struggles, wins, and insight that you have — so use it to your advantage.

Someone may have heard something 246 times, but if you can create an ah-ha moment in someone's life, you WILL become their go-to person.

I know you've met horrific trainers before who have clients that would take a bullet for them because they are THEIR expert and don't want to look for anyone else.

You DO NOT have to be the most sought-after expert in the

world to create content. Use your own experiences, stories, and ideas. People will connect better and love you for it.

## My Life Is Boring...
## No One Wants To Listen To Me

Almost everyone I know gets bored with their life, but that's because it's normal for you, but it isn't for your readers.

If you work from home and don't get out much, you can still do and say things that are interesting.

… Maybe you travel more in one month that some of your readers have in the last 5 years.

... Maybe you throw on cartoons in the morning while people are sitting in bumper to bumper traffic.

... Maybe you just finished getting some morning sex while people are filling a stupid printer with paper.

... Maybe you get to go to the gym in the middle of your day when it's dead quiet because you can do anything you want.

When you take a step back, you can find interesting things. Look at your hobbies, favorite TV shows, and movies, stories from your childhood, plans to travel, crazy people in the grocery store.

If all else fails, pick up some new skills and hobbies so you're not so boring ;)

There are two types of people in this world:

## Type #1: Publicly expresses their disgust with life and how it's "unfair."

They announce their decision to do the right thing by cutting the negativity from their life or how easy it would be for them to do X if someone hands them Y. But, nothing ever changes.

## Type #2. They just do things

They act first and ask questions later. They don't complain about their situation and make up excuses.

Instead, they're always on the offensive rather than the defensive.

Be the second type. There will be days you don't want to write, learn, study or do things to move your business forward, but the more you do it, the easier it becomes.

Next thing you know, you're way ahead of everyone else because you did the work even on days you didn't feel like it.

Now you'll be way ahead of the game because you won't make up excuses for the ones you read in this chapter that most of other trainers will make.

## COPY CLIFF NOTES

The actions are pretty simple when we wrap up this lesson:

- Just write
- Use infotainment
- Be authentic
- Use stories and examples from your life
- Be more interesting

Get instant access to bonus templates, worksheets, and notes (worth $147) visit www.WhyDoYouHateMoneyBook.com

# The Most Common Fitness Marketing Mistakes

*"Make it simple. Make it memorable. Make it inviting to look at. Make it fun to read."*

— Leo Burnett

When I was 17 years old, I was in the market for a car after wrecking my first one.

… Listen, it wasn't my fault, a large tree jumped in the middle of the road during a snowstorm.

At the time, I didn't have much money saved up and ended up buying an old Chrysler for $1200. It was a decent chunk of change for me at the time.

The musty burgundy Chrysler felt like a boat, but I didn't have many choices for my budget. The next day, I brought it in for inspection and found out there was a crack in the engine, and it was slowly but surely leaking oil.

I called the dealership I got the car from, and their response was something along the lines of "Haaahaaaa… no, give backs."

Now, anytime I go to make a significant purchase like that again, I always think the seller is hiding something from me and trying to pull a fast one.

Growing up, if I wanted something, I had to save my money and buy it myself. So, I always had older cars because that's what I was able to afford.

This leads me to have car buying experiences like this and multiple cars just breaking down on me.

Now, if I'm buying a car, I want to know that it is safe and reliable. I also want to know that if there is ever a problem with a car, it will be under warranty.

Merely offering me a warranty to put my mind at ease, so something like that doesn't happen again is a deal closer. I want to know I am going to be taken care of and I'm not going to make another decision that I'm going to regret.

The reason I'm telling you this story is because my terrible car-buying experience has left me with a sour taste in my mouth. To this day, buying a car is something I dread.

I've yet to come out of the experience without feeling like I'm being screwed over, but that's because none of them covered these common marketing mistakes.

This chapter will cover the top fitness marketing mistakes so you can make your customer experience seamless and painless.

# You Avoid Questions, Negative Emotions And Pain

Anytime your customer wants to buy something; they replay their purchasing experiences loaded with emotion and outcomes.

Most of the time they're bad, and it's your job to let them know that this is different.

I used to make the mistake of avoiding negative emotions because I thought by mentioning those things I was going to put those thoughts into my prospects minds. The truth is, they're already on their minds.

Don't make the same mistake I did.

Your prospect is already having a negative conversation in their mind, and it's your job to join the conversation that's already taking place and flip the script by helping them get what they want.

If you can get your prospect to believe that you understand what they feel like and what they are going through, they will be more open to listen, learn, and buy from you instead of someone else.

The last thing you want your reader to do is to leave with unanswered questions. Instead, you want to address and answer them.

They need to know who the product is perfect for if it's

going to help them, and their fears of getting screwed over are addressed.

You want to think of every possible objection your customer may have and address them in your writing.

If you were having a sales conversation, you could simply say "ok, if I can take care of all these issues, would you be interested in buying?" They'd say yes, and you would proceed to knock them off one by one, but you don't have that luxury in writing.

People are skeptical of getting screwed over, and rightfully so, but convincing them isn't the hard part.

The hard part is making them feel comfortable enough to overcome the objections and criticism they might get from their spouse, boss, neighbor, and friends...especially if they fail.

You can do this a few ways:

- tell a story
- use a testimonial
- explain a case study
- directly answer questions in a Q & A fashion
- restate or refer to the guarantee you're offering

It's your job to sell based on emotion but to also justify their purchase with logic.

This way they can use that same logic to fight off the critics in their lives who judge them and give them crap for trying to solve their problem after they've already failed.

## Not Believing In The Product You Sell

You can't sell using only logic.

Good salesmanship includes rational and emotional reasons. We know people buy on emotion but use rationale to explain their buying decisions to the "others" in their lives.

If you want to get someone to marry you, are you going to give them a list of reasons why marrying you is the logical choice?

> *"Listen, I don't care how you feel about me,*
> *but this marriage just makes sense, ok!?"*

We all know how that's going to end.

Instead, you sell yourself and the idea of a fruitful and beautiful life together filled with love, passion, and happiness or in some cases money, luxury and limitless material items.

If you have a problem selling, there's a good chance you don't believe in what you're selling, and it will be obvious in your writing with words like maybe, kind of, sort of, hopefully.

One of my favorite copywriters John Carlton calls this 'selling from your heels'. **DO NOT do this**.

You have to stand behind and believe in what you're selling if you want to do this the right way.

If you don't fully believe in what you're selling you need to make it better or become an affiliate/joint-venture partner with someone who does have a fantastic offer.

People are looking for a solution to their problems, and if you have that answer, you have a moral obligation to get that solution into their hands.

But, don't stress out if you struggle with this concept because most people do. In fact, Craig Ballantyne and Bedros Keuilian, two of the most successful fitness entrepreneurs, have admittedly struggled with this in the past. Now, they're some of the best closers in the game because they believe with 100% certainty that they have the best solution for their prospect's problems.

If you can't get behind your product/services, you can bet your ass they're going to go someplace else and most likely get ripped off by a terrible trainer who just wants to get them signed up with their multi-level-marketing scheme. That's how you have to look at it.

If you can't view what you're selling as something that is genuinely going to help someone, then you need to solve that problem first.

- Have one explicit action to take
- Sell the benefit, concept, big idea NOT the features

- Don't argue or fight, get them on your side by agreeing and saying "Yes."

Over the course of the book, I dig into each of them much more; but when it comes down to it, you're still selling to a human being with desires and natural instincts.

Know your customers, what they want, how you can help them, and convey that message in a clear and concise way, and confidently present your product as the solution to their problem.

## Your Stories Aren't Clear

Anytime you tell a personal story you need to make it crystal clear why your reader should care.

I'll never forget this lesson because it's the only time I ever appreciated unsolicited advice.

I wrote an article called "I Love This Woman: But She's Not My Fiancé" that got picked up and reposted by other sites.

After I posted the article to Facebook, I got a private message from Derek Halpern, the founder of Social Triggers.com.

Derek is someone I have looked up to and learned from for years. He buttered me up with a smooth opening: "you're a good writer" and followed up with "unsolicited advice"... which I was happy to accept.

Derek went on to teach me a valuable marketing lesson:

*"... Whenever you use a personal story, end it with why they should care and make it crystal clear. It can even be the same message, just make it 100 percent clear to them what the message is."*

All I did was change a few sentences, but it ultimately changed the closing of the article.

Changing the closing was an iron-clad example that no one cares about you, they care about themselves. Or in this case, no one cared about me.

People want to know how you can help them and it's your job to show the benefits they are going to get working with you.

This is how most gyms and trainers royally screw up their "About me" pages.

They're flooded with certifications, degrees, testimonials that aren't relatable, what books they've read, how much weight they've lost, and a bunch of other things that don't mean anything to the reader.

**Here's a good rule to follow:** When talking about yourself dig deep into agonizing pain, struggles, depression, and other feelings your reader gets defensive about if they feel like you're calling them out.

When it comes time to turn the story around (and go from pain to pleasure) turn the story around and make your reader the hero and focus of the story, not you. By flipping the story to your reader, they connect better and become more emotionally tied to the benefits.

You can still write stories about yourself to teach lessons and tell stories, but always, relate it back to a positive outcome or solution for your reader.

## You Write To Impress Which Makes It Confusing

*Don't sacrifice clarity to show off a big vocabulary. As Kerouac said, "One day I will find the right words, and they will be simple."*

You want your writing to feel like a personal conversation which is why good marketers don't write to impress their readers, friends, and peers.

They write to inform, educate, help, and promote action which means, no more bragging about yourself unless what you're saying is essential or directly relatable to your reader.

Don't use big words and technical terms that your customer may not know because you'll only confuse them or even worse, make them feel stupid.

Relate things like testimonials, personal results, and stories directly back to how it can help your prospect, so they realize you're the person for the job. No bragging necessary.

Have you ever noticed the best speakers are the ones who make you feel like it's just you and them in the room having a conversation?

You want your writing to feel personal, and you can do this by picturing you and your reader having a face to face conversation.

**Use more:** I, me, you, and we.

**Use less:** you all, everyone, you guys, etc.

Get good at communicating a personal message to the right people, and you will have a very successful career in the fitness industry or any other industry and relationship in your life.

## COPY CLIFF NOTES

1) Answer questions and show empathy

2) Follow the principles of good salesmanship and sell something you believe in

3) Whenever you tell a personal story, make it crystal clear why they should care

4) Make your message feel personal and seamless to read

Get instant access to bonus templates, worksheets, and notes (worth $147) visit www.WhyDoYouHateMoneyBook.com

# How To Use Kickass Copywriting To Make Loads Of Cash Without Being Salesly

*"The most powerful element in advertising is the truth."*
— William Bernbach

Copywriting is the ability to communicate a message and get a result which usually follows this simple formula: Make a promise, prove the promise, and ask for an action.

If you can grasp the concept that your prospect doesn't want what you're selling, they just want the result that it gives them, you'll never go hungry again. But if you don't, all the complicated marketing funnels and ninja marketing hacks will never amount to anything.

Good marketing makes your prospect feel like you're good friends with a juicy secret to tell them, so they eagerly lean in to make sure no one else hears.

When you write copy, you're tapping into your customer's emotional bank account which can be taxing and painful. It's personal, emotional, and it isn't always pretty.

# The Slippery Slope: Keep Attention By Being Interesting

Picture them reading with their cursor on the 'X' and one foot out the door because your readers are always one step away from leaving.

There's no shortage of crappy information out there so your readers are ALWAYS skeptical of what you have to say and why they should stick around to hear you say it.

They've been screwed before, and they think you're going to do it too, so they're looking for the angle, the tricks, and the real truth.

Here are a few ways to create a slippery slope that gets readers to slide down the page and keep reading:

- Be engaging
- Tell great stories
- Make it easy to read and understand
- Appeal to their hopes, dreams, and desires
- Use attention-grabbing headlines, sub-headlines, hooks and offers

No matter who you are writing for, you are interrupting their life, and they're going to be skeptical; and it's your job to find their biggest problem and let them know you can solve it.

A slippery slope keeps their attention high and engaged which is hard to do in the busy world we live in today.

Later in this book, I show you how to create the ultimate slippery slope with transitional words, page formatting, questions, and other copywriting hacks.

## Write Like A Casual Conversation

School taught me to write in a stiff, cold, emotionless, confusing and boring way. Then they hammered this lesson home in graduate school.

Your writing should sound like a conversation between two people, not a vocabulary pissing contest. An easy way to write casual copy is to record yourself explaining your product or service to a friend then use a transcription service like Rev.com to turn the audio or video into text.

From there, spice it up with "power words" (we'll cover them soon), make sure you have the main components of a sales message intact, and you're set.

This is a much better alternative than writing like a robot or sounding like you have a stick up your ass.

## Speak To ONE Person And Solve Their Biggest Problem

There is a famous quote by Ernest Hemingway saying "as a writer you should not judge. You should understand."

This is where you find your 'Average Joe' and connect with him using a heartfelt message. Not only do you need to know who Average Joe is, but you want to know what he needs to hear to feel good about buying from you.

In the next few chapters, I'm going to show you how you can learn everything you ever need to know about Joe's hopes, dreams, desires, fears, barriers, and so much more. Which means, you should also get an excellent idea of what questions are going on in their head as they're reading.

When you do that correctly, you'll not only know what to give them to help, but how to communicate with them and how to answer any objections they're going to have.

I know what you're thinking…"I can help everyone." Listen, you may be able to help everyone but by trying to appeal to everyone you appeal to no one. Instead, you want to become the go-to person.

The Boss.
The Leader.
The Shot Caller.

… The person that people say "Hey, I have a guy for that."

By narrowing your audience down as much as possible and speaking to your "Average Joe", you're becoming 'the guy.'

## Features Tell, Benefits Sell

I spent years spinning my wheels and missing out on thousands of dollars trying to sell prospects features, instead of benefits.

Most of your clients don't care about the how or what you use (the vehicle) to get them to their results (the destination.) They just want to arrive at the destination.

It's crucial for you to understand the difference between features and benefits because benefits are the things that sell.

**<u>Features</u> are tangible things**
**<u>Benefits</u> are what it does for someone**

You don't buy a car from the guy who spits tech features and specs.

You buy the car from the guy who sells you the picture of feeling like a badass when you hear the engine roar after punching the gas in your brand new Camaro.

Let's say you offer a 6-week transformation program.

The features could include: unlimited group training sessions, a nutrition guide, home workouts, warm up guide, and accountability

The benefits could include: Losing 15+ pounds of fat and learning how to keep it off for the rest of your life.

This is a quick exercise you can use to turn features into benefits, this way you're able to relate what you're selling to your prospect in a way they understand and that fits their desires.

First, Create a table and list the features. Next, ask yourself the following questions:

> What does it do?
>
> Why is it better?
>
> What is the problem?
>
> What does this solve?
>
> How does it make your life easier?

Finally, add the benefit of that feature. Once you connect the dots, you'll be able to show your readers how it helps. Don't make the mistake of thinking because it's easy for you to understand and is a "no-brainer"; your prospects feel the same way because that's rarely the case.

*"Hair coloring isn't about looking younger. It's about self-esteem.*
*Cameras aren't about pictures.*
*They're about stopping time and holding life as the sands run out."*

*"Hey Whipple, Squeeze This"* by Luke Sullivan

You sell solutions to problems and outcomes for products or services because your prospects want the final result the person will get from using it.

How do they feel?

Who do they become?

How will people treat them after getting this result?

The sizzle makes what you have unique, and someone should buy from you instead of some Instagram trainer with razor-sharp abs.

It can be a slew of different things, but the most common is being able to get them the result easier, faster, better, cheaper, simpler and with a unique approach or mechanism (which you'll learn about later.)

Find your sizzle now and reap the rewards of your delicious steak after.

## Get Action On A Specific Outcome

You should ALWAYS be writing with a single action in mind for your prospect to take because that's the goal of direct response marketing, remember!?

To be clear, the action doesn't have to be to buy something. It can be:

*"Watch the full video here."*

*"Read the rest of the story here."*

*"Sign up to get your free cheat sheet."*

*"Check out my favorite meme of all time."*

*… or hundreds of others*

Always make sure you have a single call to action even if it's to: like, share, comment.

Not only does this get your readers used to taking action, but it also speeds up the relationship and trust building process; and if you're using this on social media, it helps your posts get seen by more people.

I'll get much deeper into the entire sales process later in this book, but for now, I want you to take a look from a 50,000-foot view.

If you are trying to make a sale, you need to make sure you cover the basics of a sales message. Again, I first heard John Carlton reference this as Salesmanship 101 which explains:

- Who you are?
- What you have to sell?
- How is it going to help them?
- What is the next step to buy?

The best part is, if you do your customer research, (like I will show you) you already know what they want. Now all you have to do is speak directly to the reader and find the hidden benefit.

A hidden benefit is something your prospect desperately wants but doesn't come out and say.

For example; I know a lot of gym owners who love to play golf. These owners grow their team and put systems in place, so they have more time to play golf. Knowing this about your prospect could allow you to speak to their real desire of playing golf whenever and wherever they want, instead of focusing on the 'systems' and 'leads' you can bring them... because ultimately, they just want to play more golf.

The better you know your prospect, the better chance you have connected with them.

## Overcome Hurdles And Gain Trust

Can you jump through the high hurdles, tiny hoops, and molten hot lava pits to answer your prospects questions and put their minds at ease?

We're all human, so we have a few common buying objections which pop up in our minds:

"It won't work for me."

"I don't believe you."

"What happens if I don't like it?"

"Why should I listen to you?"

"Am I going to get ripped off?"

"You don't understand my problem."

The worst thing you can do is avoid their objections because if you do, your prospect will leave and go somewhere else. Not only is it your job is to acknowledge them, but it's your job to answer them as well.

An excellent way to speed up the relationship building

process and overcome objections is to give them something that will help solve their biggest problem.

This is known as an 'ethical bribe' or a 'lead magnet' because you are exchanging an email address, phone number, name, address, attention.

Most importantly they are giving you their TRUST that you can help them.

Again, your ethical bribe should solve their biggest problem and can be delivered many different ways. This is why knowing your audience will determine what's best for them.

For example, extremely busy people who want to lose a few pounds don't want to spend hours sifting through "The Ultimate Guide To Single Digit Body Fat."

Instead, they are happier to exchange their trust for something short and actionable like cheat sheets, checklists, templates and things they can efficiently use right away.

Here are a few ideas for popular ethical bribes to offer your prospect in exchange for their email or other information:

- *Checklists & Cheat sheets*
- *How-to Video*
- *Q&A Video*
- *Case study & testimonials*
- *Cheat sheet*
- *Course*

- *Scripts*
- *Templates*
- *Challenge*
- *Ebook*
- *Transcription*
- *List of resources*
- *Infographic or Diagram*

Get this right and you'll have no problem trading your prospect's attention and trust for the thing that is going to help them.

## Science of Persuasion: The Six Rules

In Dr. Robert Cialdini's book *Influence: The Psychology of Persuasion*, he lays out six persuasion rules.

If you take a look back at interactions you've had in your past that have led to BIG buying decisions, I'm sure you'll notice most of these rules were included:

1) Reciprocation
2) Commitment and Consistency
3) Social Proof
4) Liking
5) Authority
6) Scarcity

The more rules of persuasion you can display in your copy and interactions, the more likely your reader will turn into a buyer and fan for life.

I highly recommend you pick up a copy of Influence and dig into each rule plus all of the other invaluable information inside.

## COPY CLIFF NOTES

Overcome hurdles and build trust with your reader by speaking directly to them and making them feel connected and understood. Do this by using the following techniques:

1) *The Slippery Slope*

2) *Write 'Casual Copy'*

3) *Write To ONE Person*

4) *Features Tell, Benefits Sell*

5) *Get Action On A Specific Outcome*

6) *Overcoming Hurdles And Gain Trust*

7) *Dr. Cialdini's Six Rules of Persuasion*

Clean up your marketing with these seven tips so you can make loads of cash without feeling like a sellout.

Get instant access to bonus templates,
worksheets, and notes (worth $147) visit
www.WhyDoYouHateMoneyBook.com

# Mind Reading:
# The Lazy (But Genius) Way To
# Write Words That Sell

*"The vast majority of products are sold because of the need
for love, the fear of shame, the pride of achievement, the
drive for recognition, the yearning to feel important, the
urge to look attractive, the lust for power, the longing
for romance, the need to feel secure, the terror of facing
the unknown, the lifelong hunger for self-esteem and
so on. Emotions are the fire of human motivation, the
combustible force that secretly drives most decisions to buy.
When your marketing harnesses those forces correctly you
will generate explosive increases in response."*

— Gary Bencivenga

I have a secret to tell you…

People don't buy things for what they are; they buy them for
who and what they become from what you're selling.

That's why no one cares about a 6-week workout program

with a diet plan. Instead, they want whatever the results of what that's going to be.

A lot of trainers think their clients are different, but when we get down to the bottom of it, we're all human which gives us the same primal needs, wants, and desires as other humans.

| | |
|---|---|
| *Sex* | *Love* |
| *Pride* | *Health* |
| *Wealth* | *Status* |
| *Intimacy* | *Purpose* |
| *Approval* | *Respect* |
| *Security* | *Association* |
| *A better deal* | *Self improvement* |

It's always about an increase in status and how they view themselves or how they believe others perceive them. Marketing genius Russell Brunson does a fantastic job of making this point clear in his book Expert Secrets. On a similar note Jon Goodman, creator of the Personal Trainer Development Center does an excellent job of explaining this concept in regards to social media in his book Viralnomics.

As humans, we want to feel special, and we want what we can't or don't have. It's been this way since long before you were born and will continue to work this way.

This all comes down to a straightforward question: "Is this going to add or take away from my life?"

If your prospect answers that question with a yes, you get a customer, but if they don't see the value, they walk away and find the next person who knows them better and can increase their status.

The best part is, the customer research phase is annoying as hell so most people will skip this part because they're lazy, which is good news for you and I because it allows us to discover "the hidden benefit" most important to them.

The hidden benefit your customer is looking for will take some digging to find, but if you can nail this, you'll be able to connect with your prospects better than you've ever imagined.

Very rarely will someone spill their guts to you and tell you everything you need to know, so if you're doing in-person interviews and sales calls, this takes a lot of poking, prodding, and redirecting of questions.

To do this, question everything, even to the point of sounding like a broken record.

Ask: "Why? Why? Why? Why? Why? Why?"

… over and over again until that sneaky truth bomb slips out, almost undetected.

Remember, nine times out of ten this relates back to an increase in status, but this is your reader's perception, worldview, emotions, beliefs, attitudes, frustrations, from their eyes. Not yours.

Here are my top 11 ways to eavesdrop on my prospects, learn what they want, and find the exact words and phrases they're using:

1) **Groups & Forums:** get active and ask questions or lurk in the shadows to see how people interact and ask questions.

2) **Surveys:** an excellent place to ask your list what they want, like, struggle with, etc.

3) **Amazon:** check out reviews, best sellers, also liked

4) **Google Search:** find pretty much anything known to mankind

5) **Live Events:** What are people paying to go to, what presentations get positive reactions, what kind of questions do they ask?

6) **Similar Web:** check out websites that have related content and see where they get traffic, referrals, etc.

7) **The Players:** Who are the big players in the industry, what are they doing, how are they doing it, and why are they crushing it.

8) **Quora and Reddit:** Topics and questions in exact phrases in threads created by people looking to solve a problem

9) **Keyword Searchers:** find out what buzzwords and phrases people use to search

10) **Industry Popular Magazines:** What are people reading?

11) **Video or in-person consultations:** questions, problems, and struggles coming straight from the horse's mouth which you can use, word for word in your writing.

All you have to do is find where the fish are swimming and learn from them because they already did the work for you.

Not only that but now you can use these exact words and phrases when speaking to your prospects.

## Players Play... Find The Shepherd For Inspiration

Speaking of doing the work for you, The Shepherds are the leaders in your niche.

First, let me make this crystal clear.

This does NOT mean you can steal someone else's work and pass it off as your own. Not only is trying to be someone else an exhausting business model but it's morally wrong and completely illegal.

Just don't do it, ok?

Now that we got that out of the way. If you can find the shepherds who are already leading people you want to help and are doing it well, you're in luck because you can leverage their success for the success of your own.

They've already created cult-like tribes of loyal fans who will passionately follow them and fight for them at the drop of a hat. If they have a solid foundation, all you have to do is look at what they're doing and what is working.

Again, **DO NOT STEAL THEIR SHIT**

What you're doing is looking to see what they've done that has been a big hit and what you can use for ideas and inspiration not blatantly rip them off. They don't have to offer the same thing as you, but their audience has to be like yours. Otherwise, this doesn't work.

Study the feedback and comments they're getting and use this to understand your readers and humans in general

Watch, read, learn, and listen for inspiration *(but still be you.)*

## COPY CLIFF NOTES

Make sure you dig into the customer research phase. Not only will this help your writing come across as more genuine and authentic, but it will help you write copy that sells.

- *Surveys*
- *Amazon*
- *Live Events*
- *Similar Web*
- *The Players*
- *Google Search*
- *Groups & Forums*
- *Quora and Reddit*
- *Keyword Searchers*
- *Industry Popular Magazines*
- *Video or in-person consultations*

Learn from what successful people like you (or talking to your audience) do but develop your own words, phrases, sayings, style, and personality to connect with your audience.

Get instant access to bonus templates, worksheets, and notes (worth $147) visit www.WhyDoYouHateMoneyBook.com

# How To Make Your Reader Feel Like They're The Only Person In The Room

*"I don't know how to speak to everybody, only to somebody."*
— Howard Gossage

Good copy speaks to one person, and one person only (remember Average Joe from a couple of chapters ago?)

Again, you want it to feel like an intimate written conversation, and I can't remember the last time I had a private discussion with nine completely different people at the same time.

It's time to create your ideal customer (aka your avatar.) This is your perfect prospect based on the research you just did, plus a few more goodies like:

Name, age, sex, family size, income, how many hours per week do they work, what are their interests and hobbies, where do they live, what are their values, what TV shows do they watch, etc.

Demographics are an excellent place to start because they help us paint a picture of a single person in our head, but they don't do much without some more digging.

You'll have to do some more research to get into their minds and find out what makes your prospect tick. Their hopes, dreams, desires, anger, pain, failures, biggest barriers, roadblocks, uncertainties. These are the things that make them stare at the ceiling worrying all night:

*"Am I ever going to get a date?"*
*"Am I going to be alone for the rest of my life?"*
*"Am I always going to be afraid of defending myself?"*
*"Am I going to die young like my father, his father, and his father"*

People come to you to lose weight for a variety of different reasons, and it's your job to know **WHY**.

Meet Nancy, a 44-year-old mother of 4 who desperately wants to lose weight. She went to the doctor who expressed his concern for her health. Every single one of her parents and grandparents passed away from heart disease. She has a family she loves, a husband who adores her, and a life she doesn't want to leave. She needs to lose weight to be around for them and watch them grow old.

Meet Hank, a 30-year old professional video gamer who looks like Ryan Gosling's overweight stepbrother. He just got divorced. He returned from winning a gaming tournament and took home a cash pot of $285,000 big ones to find his wife sleeping with their pool-boy. All while Hank was killing zombies in the virtual world. Hanks wants to get jacked, shredded, and look and feel healthier because he's ready to get back into the dating world and slay it like Ryan G.

That's a decent start, but you need to dig even deeper than that.

… Nancy is terrified she's not going to wake up one morning. She wants to be a grandmother more than anything, and if things continue to go the way they have been, she's afraid she'll never see that day. She's scared out of her mind every time she goes to the doctors and fears that the next visit is the day she gets diagnosed with heart disease just like everyone else in her family, and won't live long enough to spend with her husband and kids.

… Hank is angry, upset, and spiteful. His pride was crushed by the woman he loved who made him feel like he had no purpose. He craves love, purpose, and respect. He wants it all back and to share that intimacy with a beautiful woman, but he can't do that until he feels more confident about his body. He wants control of his life and fears that if he doesn't change his unhealthy habits, he'll be alone for the rest of his life.

You see, it's not all sunshine and rainbows here. To sell more, you have to care more, and there's no way to get around it. This is what a lot of trainers get all wrong.

It's up to you to understand what your prospects deep dark

fears, desires, and frustrations are, and offer them a solution coming from a place of understanding, not judgment.

When you do your research, you're going to find the answers to a lot of these questions if you're looking in the right place. You're going to get surface level answers and REAL answers... you're after the real answers because these lead to solutions.

Surface level answers are when people answer questions but are timid, shy, and in fear that they're going to offend someone or be judged when they tell the truth of what they want. So they give answers they think are politically correct or answers that you want to hear.

We need more. You can do a few in-person or video interviews to have people open up a bit more so you can get to the juicy stuff. This is where you're able to dig deeper and find out why.

## COPY CLIFF NOTES

Here are seven questions you can ask yourself or your prospect to dive deep into their human psyche and return home with GOLD that will sell itself:

1) *What pisses them off when they see or hear?*

2) *What do they wish would happen more than anything?*

3) *What has to happen for them to feel good about buying?*

4) *What are they afraid is going to happen if they do say yes?*

5) *What gives them anxiety when they go to bed or wake up?*

6) *What are they afraid will happen if they continue down the path they are on?*

7) *What has happened when they've tried to fix this before?*

If you want to dig even deeper invest in Dan Kennedy's book 'The Ultimate Sales Letter' where he explains 10 questions where he digs even deeper.

Remember, at first you're going to get a lot of surface level answers, but the deeper you can dig and the more pain you can find, the easier it will be to emphasize and connect with your readers. Use these questions as a starting point.

Use these questions as a starting point.

Get instant access to bonus templates,
worksheets, and notes (worth $147) visit
www.WhyDoYouHateMoneyBook.com

# Invaluable Marketing Lessons From Learning How To Backflip

*"The consumer isn't a moron; she is your wife. You insult her intelligence if you assume that a mere slogan and a few vapid adjectives will persuade her to buy anything."*
— David Ogilvy

I've wanted to learn how to backflip for as long as I can remember.

Since I was a kid I've been jealous of street performers, break dancers, and gymnasts who can flip, fly, and spin through the air like it is nothing.

This wasn't the first time I set a goal to learn how to backflip. In fact, just two years before I said the same thing. I was living in NYC and went to 3 different gymnastics gyms in the city. All of which spoke to me like I was doing gymnastics for 15 years.

Why?

Poor communication. No, TERRIBLE communication.

Being in the fitness industry for 10+ years I experienced both fantastic and crap coaches.

Keep in mind, I coached in the fitness industry for over 10+ years, and physical activity was always a part of my life. Up to this point, I already accomplished what most people would consider "impressive" physical feats like earning my black belt when I was a kid, dunked a basketball as a short 5'9" dude, deadlifted 600 pounds, box jumped 63.5" inches, competed in amateur boxing, and more.

On top of that, I was certified as a coach by world recognized organizations and worked with some of the top coaches for years at this point. Still, these gymnastics coaches had no idea how to coach me.

The reason was simple. These coaches didn't give a crap about who they were talking to, aka, their audience. And I'm someone who WANTS to be coached and enjoys getting coached.

If I was an elite-level gymnast, I'm sure their coaching would have been incredible, but that wasn't me.

You see, good coaches are tough to come by… just like marketing.

I'm talking about actually being a good coach. There's a big difference between knowing what you're talking about and being able to communicate it in a way that your audience understands.

That's what great marketing does.

It all comes down to being able to communicate with your audience.

Who are they?

How do they talk?

What do they feel?

Where are they now?

Where do they want to go?

What are they motivated by?

What's their biggest struggle?

As you can see, this is more than age, sex, race, pain, pleasures, and other surface-level crap. Lucky for me, I found a coach who can do that, and I quickly learned to backflip because of it.

He listened, he answered questions, explained what was happening, brought me through the process, and met me at my level, not someone else's.

## COPY CLIFF NOTES

You can have the best product or service in the world, but if you can't communicate with someone in a way they'll understand, you're NEVER going to be successful.

- People can't know how great your product or service is if they don't understand what and how you can help them.

- They will never care how much you know until they know how much you care.

- They will never understand why you're the best fit for them opposed to some $19/month gym membership.

If you want to change lives, you owe it to yourself and your clients to learn the principles of marketing and copywriting. Period.

And not the stuff that makes you feel icky… the good stuff.

Get instant access to bonus templates,
worksheets, and notes (worth $147) visit
www.WhyDoYouHateMoneyBook.com

# Hook Your Reader For Good With The Perfect Big Idea

*"Don't tell me the moon is shining; show me the glint of light on broken glass."*

— Anton Chekhov

Now it's time to grab your reader by the throat and pull them into your writing.

The big idea is: what hooks your reader and sucks them in so you can offer a new or different opportunity that solves a problem, provides a secret, debunks a myth that has been holding them back or make a bold promise that is going to help them.

When it comes down to it, your big idea will always increase "status" in some way. In the book 'Breakthrough Copywriting' World's Greatest Copywriting Coach David Garfinkel lists the seven main reasons people buy:

1)  Make money
2)  Save money
3)  Save time

4) Save effort

5) Improve health

6) Increase pleasure

7) Eliminate pain

This is why it becomes important to know what motivates your customers. Some people care much more about making money than saving it.

You want things to be specific and for people to care about what you're selling. You do this by presenting a new opportunity. In the book, Expert Secrets, Russell Brunson talks about submitting an offer as a unique (and new) opportunity instead of an improved offer of what is already available.

Why?

Because new opportunities spark curiosity and allow them to escape reality and arrive in the place they dream about. It's something new, different, and exciting that they haven't tried in the past.

When you frame something like a new opportunity, you're less likely to get resistance that comes along with the reader trying and failing before.

This is the same as selling the cure, instead of a prevention. Our human nature makes us more inclined to buy things that cure our problems rather than something that may or may not prevent a future issue.

It's the big idea behind your entire offer.

**Example #1:** Be happier is very general when compared to being a happier and healthier dad with no knee pain in 30 minutes per week (which is more specific.) A dad who wants to be able to play with his kids without being in pain but is busy and doesn't want to spend tons of time in the gym.

**Example #2:** The magic in Domino's offer to deliver pizza in less than 30 minutes or else it's free was brilliant because they did their research. They found that people were fed up with not knowing when their pizza would be delivered, and they solved the problem.

**Example #3:** A headline from world-class copywriter John Carlton sparks curiosity with an unordinary idea. If an old guy with arthritis who is out of shape can beat pros, why can't you?

> *"How Does An Out-of-shape 55 Year Old Golfer,*
> *Crippled By Arthritis And 71 Lbs. Overweight,*
> *Still Consistently Humiliate PGA Pros In*
> *Head To Head Matches By Hitting Every Tee Shot*
> *Farther And Straighter Down The Fairway?"*

When I was a personal trainer, I used to think I was selling workouts, training, diets. I see this same mistake over and over again.

The truth is, I was selling security and peace of mind helping them get the results they wanted without getting injured or wasting their time and money on things that didn't work.

## Someone Solve This Problem For Me!

Ever since I was a little kid, I get motion sickness like a son of a bitch. Cars, boats, planes, trains: you name it, and I get sick on it.

Anyone who gets sick like this knows how much of a pain in the ass it can be, and it's such a crappy feeling. Dramamine works sometimes but it sure as hell ain't magic.

But if you had a magic pill that I could take and never get sick again, I'd buy it.

So here's a bottle of Dramamine for $10 bucks to MAYBE prevent me from getting sick when I am traveling, I'll buy it, but the most I'd pay for something like this would be $30 bucks or so because it doesn't even work all the time.

Now, if you came to me with a magic pill that would CURE my motion sickness for good… well, now I'm willing to fork out thousands… easy. No questions asked.

Here is this massive PROBLEM and inconvenience of mine and I am looking for a SOLUTION.

The thing is, it's hard to sell preventions because we all expect nothing bad to happen to us until it's too late.

I can't even count the number of client consultations I've had with people who've hurt their back picking up something off the ground, and they always finish the statement with, but I know to lift with my legs and not my back.

But now they have severe back pain and are ready to do anything to make it go away. I know because, in 2013, I herniated L5 and S1 deadlifting. I had to sit in the middle seat on a red-eye back home to Pennsylvania and was in so much pain I would have sold my soul to the devil to make it go away.

My point is, find a hook based on a cure, not prevention.

## COPY CLIFF NOTES

Here are 5 Attention Grabbing Hooks to spark ideas for your big idea.

1) **The painful truth:** the harsh reality which they've believed in isn't real and is the thing holding them back, i.e., you don't need more information, you need a simple plan that's easy to execute, just like this.

2) **Fight the enemy:** Get on the same team with your reader by talking about the lies, scams, and cons of their worst enemy, i.e., in health and fitness this is typically big pharma, supplement companies, $5 templated workout programs that are garbage.

3) **Little known concept:** Secret or misunderstood idea that you can shed light on, i.e., "How To Outfox The Foxes. 263 Secrets The Law And Lawyers Don't Want You To Know!"

4) **Brand-new discovery:** A new concept, idea, or unique mechanism that allows them to do something

easier, quicker, faster, etc. i.e. P90X's 'Muscle Confusion' is a great example of this.'

5) **Unbelievable story:** A story with an exciting plot or twist that is hard to believe, i.e., Carlton's famous headline "…One-Legged Golfer Adds 50 Yards to Your Drives, Eliminates Hooks and Slices... and Can Slash Up to 10 Strokes From Your Game Almost Overnight."

You can also give a unique name to a technique, make a bold warning, or use a strong If-then statement. You'll notice there is going to be carry over between different hooks and your big idea, headline, and stories which we will dig into right now…

Get instant access to bonus templates,
worksheets, and notes (worth $147) visit
www.WhyDoYouHateMoneyBook.com

# Why Be Someone Else When You're Already The Best At Being You

*"The one thing that you have that nobody else has is you. Your voice, your mind, your story, your vision. So write and draw and build and play and dance and live as only you can."*

— Neil Gaiman

To be honest, I can't say it any better than the great Neil Gaiman did in the quote above so I'm just going to add to it.

We live in a day where so many people just copy or blatantly rip off what others are doing. There are a few problems with this.

1) It's wrong. Very very wrong.

2) It will only get you so far because you'll never develop a voice of your own and genuinely connect with your audience.

For the most part, humans are pretty smart and follow their gut instinct. How many times has something happened, but you weren't surprised because deep down you always had a funny feeling about that person? Probably a lot.

Plus you're a fool to think you can do something shady and get away with it with all the reviews and social media blast potential.

The thing is, you need to develop your voice if you want to create a following for fans and build a successful business that helps loads of people and makes money.

Do you know how people decide whether they're going to buy from you or your competitor if you have a relatively similar product?

They will buy from whoever they feel more connected to. This is harder to do when you don't have a face of the company or a persona to market from — but that's an entirely different monster in itself which is outside the scope of this book.

My good friend and mentor John Romaniello hammered this into my brain before we even met. Not only is John the most skilled writer in fitness but he's also the best storyteller and does it all in his own unique style that can NOT be replicated (although people try often.) John also happens to be the reason I dove into copywriting head first but that's a story for another time.

# I Don't Know What You're Selling But I Like You

… yea, I'll take 3.

I don't know about you, but I've never met a person who loves to say "Yes" to people they disagree with and hate even if they know they should.

Mainly because it's natural to be influenced by people we like. Remember the principles of persuasion I mentioned in Cialdini's book?

Have you ever bought something from someone because you know them, trust them and like them but have no idea what they're selling? I sure as hell have.

I bought Dan's "Thing."

Dan Meredith runs the ultra-successful, helpful, and fantastic Facebook groups "Coffee With Dan," and "Espresso With Dan."

He also happens to be friend and mentor of mine and one of the guys who convinced me to go 'all in' on my copywriting. So thanks for that buddy.

One day Dan slapped a lengthy post in the group about "his thing."

It was dirty, raunchy, provocative, witty, but didn't tell you what he was selling for 47 quid (which is ~$60 for us 'Merica folk.) It was hilarious, entertaining, and witty so of course, I bought it.

I knew Dan, liked him, and trusted him. I knew whatever it was, he was going to deliver something kickass, so I bought it along with hundreds of other people. And I was right; It ended up being Dan's new custom designed "Get Shit Done Planner."

**My point is, YOU and your personality will help you stand out and build a close-knit bond with your prospects.**

Look into your personal life to find unique interests and experiences you can weave into what you're currently doing. Like your favorite heroes, shared interests, personality traits, hobbies, experience when you were a kid, common enemies, struggles and failures, and so much more.

This will separate you from your competitors and allow you to shine bright like the north star. All of your failures, successes, and risks led you to where you are today and the type of person you are.

The best part is, no one else in this world has taken the same exact journey. Your thoughts, feelings, and actions make you unique, and finding a way to use those will speed up the relationship building and trust process with you and your prospects.

The same things that repel people who disagree with you are the things that attract people who agree with you.

A perfect example of this outside of fitness is Ryan Stewman, of The Hardcore Closer. Ryan openly talks about his time spent in prison, he's loud, he curses, and the dude just does and says off the wall things. By doing this he's built a cult following of people who either love him or hate him. Personally, I think he's awesome.

Being unique will allow you to build a cult or tribe of people who rally with you. These people are connected to one another with a similar idea or interest and led by a leader.

They've been around for millions of years, think religions, politics, sports, music, and so on. These ideas are built on hope, change, and winning, and you are that leader.

In The One Sentence Persuasion Course, persuasion expert Blair Warren states...

"People will do anything for those who encourage their dreams, justify their failure, allay their fears, confirm their suspicions, and help them throw rocks at their enemies."

This is very important to understand and beneficial if you can replicate.

## The Truth About Why People Will Pick You

In the winter of 2012, one email sent me on a 9-hour trip to spend a few hours with one of my favorite strength coaches.

I was in graduate school at the time researching my thesis: Studying the Effects of Using Chains as Variable Resistance in the Squat. So I sent an email to Louie Simmons to clear up a few questions. If you don't know who Louie Simmons of Westside Barbell is, I'll give you a little insight:

Louie is known as the Godfather of Powerlifting, and his gym is a private invite-only training facility for powerlifters. Louie's gym is known as, "The Strongest Gym In The World" and has a STRONG cult-like following. In fact, a documentary was filmed about them called "Westside vs. The World."

Louie promptly answered my questions and invited me up to the gym. I wrangled up my brother Matt for a 9-hour trip to Pennsylvania through Columbus Ohio. This was my first trip to Westside for a 2-night stay to gather some research for my thesis and then come right back home.

We ended up spending hours with Lou just hanging out and shooting the shit. He took us all out to lunch that day and did the same the following morning.

That summer I spent four months interning at Westside Barbell and saw the same story play out over and over again for lifters and coaches who visited from all over the world.

It's just what Louie did, but this is my most memorable and valuable lesson I learned from spending four months at The World's Strongest Gym...

I was learning about what motivates people to do what they do. A man like that isn't driven by money, so marketing with those things in mind for a guy like Louie would be a complete fail.

The same goes for legendary strength coaches and mentors of mine, Joe Defranco and James 'Smitty' Smith.

Instead... price, purpose, respect, and legacy are characteristics that are going to hit home for these world-class coaches.

Have you noticed the community, family, and cult that CrossFit has created?

The 'Us vs. You' mentality, the family, the friendship, the bond, the movement.

If you can create something similar to this, you will have a have a tribe that stands by our side no matter what. They will buy everything you have to offer, attend every meeting, tell all their friends, and fight for you.

I already know you've seen these people fight for days bashing CrossFit haters online because that's their family.

Find a way to create a bond like this and people won't even care what you're selling.

## COPY CLIFF NOTES

Here are a few questions for you to answer truthfully to get you started on the right path to discover how you can stand out in a crowded market:

- What do you love?

- What do you hate?

- What do you stand for and against?

- What values do you respect in others?

- What are your strengths and weaknesses?

- What will be written on your tombstone and said at your funeral?

- What are the biggest struggles/wins that made you who you are?

A few of these questions are from a program of Dan's called 'Core Story.'

Dan's training brings you step by step through a much deeper process that will allow you answer questions about yourself that can shift your perspective on life. That training completely shifted the way I viewed myself and helped change my business for the better. I highly recommend it.

Get instant access to bonus templates,
worksheets, and notes (worth $147) visit
www.WhyDoYouHateMoneyBook.com

# Storytelling Methods To Make People Fall In Love With You

*"Long before the first formal business was established the six most powerful words in any language were Let Me Tell You A Story"*
— Mathews & Wacker

It's been said that experience is the best teacher but good storytelling is a close second.

As humans, we're hardwired to listen to stories, and it's easier for us to remember complicated concepts as opposed to random facts that don't mean anything. One of the biggest reasons people won't buy from you is because they don't know, like, or trust you, but stories speed up that process.

That's why stories are the shortcut into your reader's heart. From reading this book (and life experience), you know facts tell, but stories sell because people buy on emotion, not logic.

Stories allow people to say "Here you go, take these ideas and experience them for yourself," in a Hopeful, Exciting, Amusing, Realistic, Inspiring, Engaging, Emotional,

Convincing, Captivating, Memorable, or Life-Changing way.

Good stories can skip the critical thinking phase and lead straight to taking action.

They say, "Hey, I had this problem and here's how I solved it and you can too."

If you have an idea, concept, or message that you want to get out to the world and connect with people, storytelling will be your best friend. There are three different types of learners and stories can teach them all:

1) **Auditory:** who learn from the specific words

2) **Visual:** who learn from mental pictures from stories

3) **Kinesthetic:** who connect with the emotions the stories evoke

By now you realize marketing is extraordinarily emotional and connects with your reader's deep desires even the ones people don't share out loud. This forces you to address those negative thoughts, opinions, beliefs, and biases for them. This is what I spoke about earlier about my cringeworthy car buying experiences.

The thing is, negative thoughts don't always mean something bad. In fact, bringing these negative ideas and thoughts to the front of their mind often builds rapport with your reader because they feel like you understand them instead of being some mythical creature behind a keyboard.

This allows you to connect with your reader by being vulnerable and letting them know you were scared, over-whelmed, tired, hopeless, wanted to quit, etc. You already know they're thinking it, and if you don't address it you're going to miss the emotional response, you get from excellent storytelling. This way you're able to tell your reader how bad things are, but do it in a way that they can relate to or do it from their point of view.

First, acknowledge the negative feelings and emotions.

Second, validate their feelings.

Third, use examples from yourself or someone else to talk about how bad reality is, what can continue to happen, and how it might get worse.

Next, reveal you found a solution and how you came across it.

Finally, the transition to the sale by offering to share the solution with your reader to help them solve their problem just like you did.

Stories work because people rarely argue about them even if they know they're not 100% true because it's hard to argue against someone's emotions.

# The Basics Of Storytelling

First, let's cover what makes a story a story: It has a beginning, a middle, and an end. It's not the most effective story but it's a good start, and it will allow me to prove a simple point.

Saying, "the grass was such a pain in the ass to cut" isn't a story, it's a statement. But if you said:

"The grass was such a pain in the ass to cut. I couldn't find the keys to unlock the shed, then I cut the extension cord and had to go to the store to buy a new one, and it started to rain while I was there, so I had to just sit inside of my house like a hooligan with my grass half mowed. Luckily I was able to finish the job the next day."

Right now, I want to arm you with straightforward, actionable storytelling advice so here are a few essential storytelling elements you want to be aware of:

## Give Context

Also known as the setting. Starting with context allows the listener to begin to paint a picture in their head. It gives a background, catches attention, creates interest, and gives an idea of the who, what, where, when, and what the problem is.

Context is a great place to introduce the hero and their goal (win, save the world, get the girl, etc.) which should be something they can identify with. If you're the face of your brand, it will most likely be you or a client. This is also where you're going to introduce the villain of the story which can be a rival, pestering boss, evil organization, impossible challenge, etc.

## Describe Action

Good stories involve a hero and villain face off, and in most cases, it's more than once in the story. But remember, the villain doesn't have to be another person, it can be a situation, event, organization, etc.

The action is where conflict pokes its head out and is usually where the hero fails when they first meet (or even the first few meetings.) The best and most memorable stories have some twist, surprise, action or outcome you didn't expect.

## The Result

Be sure to describe the details of who won in the end, the lesson or moral of the story and why this is important.

It may be evident to you, but your reader could be fixated on another part of the story, and ultimately gloss over the point. Not only that, but it helps reaffirm their beliefs and cements this into their head.

# Making Your Stories Even More Memorable

Using dialogue is an easy way to improve your stories and make the reader feel more connected.

Dialogue is a conversation between two or more people. When you use dialogue in your story, it makes the reader feel on the 'inside' like they are part of the event. Make sure it's about something important and relevant that moves the story forward in some way and be sure to clear up the confusion, increase suspense, strengthen a character's stance, and more.

Another quick and easy way to make a story more relatable is to use metaphors and analogies:

Using metaphors and analogies in your writing is a surefire way to stand out and attract critical attention. They help explain complex topics in a way that is relatable interesting and different.

**A metaphor** is a figure of speech that describes an object, action, or person that is not literally true and does not use the word like or as. For example; Steve is a couch potato, life is a rollercoaster, or that workout was hell

**An analogy** is a logical comparison between two things which are similar or comparable. For example: Finding a good personal trainer is like finding a needle in a haystack, My last diet was a roller coaster ride of emotions, His voice is as piercing as nails scraping down on a chalkboard.

We already speak in metaphors and analogies on a day-to-day basis so when you can add these to your stories they make your reader feel more connected to both you and the story.

Storytelling is straightforward and will never go out of style...

It's one of the most powerful skills any person can learn because it's how we connect with people. They're memorable, and people love to share great stories. You can teach, inspire, and motivate at the same time, and it works regardless of who you're talking to, where they are from, what they do, their age, or their gender.

## COPY CLIFF NOTES

Here are 13 themes for stories to get the creative juices flowing in your mind:

1) *Poor gets rich*

2) *Underdog wins*

3) *The truth about*

4) *Before And After*

5) *Secret Revealed*

6) *Man on a mission*

7) *Amazing Discovery*

8) *Loss To Redemption*

9) *Confirms existing fear*

10) *The big breakthrough*

11) *3rd Party Testimonial*

12) *Loser gets in with the crowd*

13) *Average becomes world-class*

Remember, there are no boring subjects, only boring writers, and storytellers. Don't be one of the boring ones.

Get instant access to bonus templates, worksheets, and notes (worth $147) visit www.WhyDoYouHateMoneyBook.com

# How To Write Headlines That Even Your Worst Enemy Can't Ignore

*"I re-headlined ads and increased their pull by 475%. I have a client who pays me $195,000 per year to write headlines."*

— Gary Halbert

In today's world, we are pounded continuously in the face with advertisement right hooks like you're Mike Tyson's punching bag. Some facts say you only have 3-5 seconds to grab someone's attention; and after that, they're gone.

The headline is one of the most important parts of your writing because the #1 goal for your headline is to get your prospect to read the next line. That's it. It's to get them started down the slippery slope which creates a ripple effect and the next thing they know, they're at the bottom of the page ready to take action.

A headline's primary job is to get people sucked into the piece of writing, but its role isn't to sell you on it right there because that comes later in the sales message. They're designed to stop readers in their tracks and suck them into whatever it is you have for them by making a bold promise or by arousing curiosity.

It's crucial to know your audience before you write a headline because good headlines use specific words to qualify the reader, so they know it's specifically for them.

For example: if you're selling a health supplement that helps hair growth, you're not just going to state a general benefit like 'grow hair.'

Instead, you want to make your headline more specific, like:

*"Doctors Discover Magic Pill*
*Helping Balding Men All Around The United States*
*Regrow A Full Head Of Hair"*

A headline like this catches interest, shows expert authority from "doctors," states who this ad is for, and what the benefit is. All headlines don't have to be long like this. I'll be giving you headline templates you can use shortly.

And no, I didn't write that headline because I am bald and want a full a head of hair. I wrote that headline because I see men every single day fighting to hold onto every last strand of hair instead of just shaving it.

One of the best things you can do before writing headlines is to read ones already written, so anytime you come across an article, advertisement, email, or sales message take a screenshot and save it to a swipe file. This way you can take a quick look through to get your creative juices flowing and take a different spin on things.

People who write headlines for magazines like this, get paid the big bucks because the companies know that NOTHING gets read unless the headline does its job and sucks the reader in.

Here are some excellent resources for proven headlines:

- Star
- Swiped.co
- Readers Digest
- National Enquirer
- Top magazines in your niche

*… "But Joey, these headlines are so cliche."*

For the most part, you're 100% right, but people speak in a cliched way, which is what makes it cliche.

For that reason, you're not taking the headlines in magazines like National Enquirer and using them word-for-word. Instead, you're taking a look at what they're doing and figuring out ways you can adapt that type of headline to your audience.

Don't do what most people do and put .2% effort into your headline. Every time you're writing headlines you should list out a bunch and keep trying different variations to make them better. If you're stuck, start with some of the 25 templates I give you below and just started writing.

The funny thing is if you start by writing terrible headlines all you have to do is write opposite of that to make it useful. It sounds simple, but once you start listing these, you'll know what I mean.

Be sure to write many headlines for every email, blog post, sales page, and social media you make. Don't half-ass this.

## COPY CLIFF NOTES

I've put together a list of 25 proven headline templates for you to use:

1) Are you [probing question]?

2) How-To [desired result]

3) Secrets of [who they admire or trust]

4) If you are [characteristic], you can [desired result]

5) Who else wants to [desired result]

6) Give Me [time] and I'll [surprising result]: *"Give Me 15 minutes 4 times per week and I'll help you lose your baby weight in 1 month"*

7) [End result] + [Time period] + [Address the objections]: *"How to make a fat burning dinner in under 15 minutes for under 6 dollars*

8) [Do Something] like [world-class example]

9) Do you recognize the [number] early warning signs of [blank]:

10) Why I [blank] and maybe you should too

11) If you don't [blank] now, you'll hate yourself later

12) The biggest like in [industry]

13) [blank] may be causing you to lose out on [desired result]

14) The ugly truth about [something they've tried and failed with]

15) What everybody ought to know about [topic]

16) Discover the [desired result] secret

17) How [something weird or different] made me [desired result]

18) How [impressive number] got [result] without [undesirable result]

19) Thousands now [do something] who never thought they could

20) Build a [desired result] you can be proud of

21) They didn't think I could [desired result], but when I did

22) If you can [blank] you can [desired result]

23) How to turn [blank] into [desired result]

24) Improve your [desired result] in [time period]

25) Get [desired result] without losing [something they don't want to sacrifice]

Get instant access to bonus templates, worksheets, and notes (worth $147) visit www.WhyDoYouHateMoneyBook.com

# Knock The Socks Off Your Readers With Hard-Hitting Bullet Points

*"When I write an advertisement, I don't want you to tell me that you find it 'creative.' I want you to find it so interesting that you buy the product."*

— David Ogilvy

In this chapter, we're going to jam on 1-3 line sentences that take a specific benefit of your product and make it stand out powerfully and excitingly.

These are known as bullet points, but just because they are bullet points doesn't mean you have to use actual bullets. Numbers work well too, but we're not interested in using them as lists to summarize things.

You're going to start using bullet points to create: excitement, anxiety, intrigue, curiosity, or a desire for more, all of which result in more sales.

Bullets are like mini-headlines and sub-headlines. In fact,

you can use the other headlines you already drafted and craft them into compelling bullet points.

Each bullet point is a mini-story that paints a specific picture in your reader's mind by using action verbs. Complicated ideas become easy to understand, boring concepts become fascinating, and the impossible becomes possible.

Here are four simple starting points for writing blood-boiling bullet points:

- **Fast, Easy, Simple, Cheap, Better, Etc:** On page 15 you'll learn the simple secret to shedding weight by making the same amount of food seem twice as much, so you're never hungry again.

- **Use Gary Halbert's famous 'So What' test to find the real benefits:** Resist the urge of listing features in your bullet points. Use legendary copywriter Gary Halberts 'So What' test to find the real benefit of a specific feature and showcase why the reader should care.

- **Create unique names:** Creating unique names *(ex. 'The Briefcase Technique' by Ramit Sethi)* improves positioning and expert status in your market. These can be little systems, techniques, or formula you add a name to, and it becomes associated with your brand.

- **Keep them consistent:** You can write long or short bullet points just be sure to keep your bullet point relatively the same length, so they flow and are easier to read.

Remember, feel free to go back to the headlines you drafted and use them as a starting point.

Now let's get into the good stuff.

At any point in time, you're going to have people reading your copy who are at different points in their lives, their struggles, and how they feel. Hell, you can catch someone first thing in the morning, and they could feel entirely different than they do after a long stressful day of work.

For that reason, they are going to have different emotions, feelings, thoughts, and beliefs surrounding your product because a single bullet point can take someone who is on the fence and not sure about buying, and knock them right off, turning them into a buyer.

That's the power of well-written bullet points. They give you the opportunity to appeal to different people.

Use these templates as a starting point to come up with AT LEAST 14 bullet points for your product or service.

## COPY CLIFF NOTES

Here are 14 bullet-point templates you can use in your copy today:

1) **# things you should know about _____**

   *7 things you should know about car dealerships before you even think about buying a new car*

2) **# simple steps to _____**

   *5 simple steps to paying off your student loan faster than everyone else*

3) **# time, gas, and money-saving tricks every _____ must know before doing _____**

   *11 time and energy saving tricks every man must know before taking a road trip*

4) **How to effortlessly _____ in half the time**

   *How to effortlessly make twice as much money in half the time as your co-workers*

5) **Give me _____ and I'll give you _____**

   *Give me 30 minutes and I'll give you an unforgettable fat loss trick*

6) **If _____ then _____**

   *If you can spare 30 minutes 3 times per week you can drop 15 pounds in 28 days*

7) **The truth about _____**

   *The truth about taxes the IRS doesn't want you to know*

8) **What to do when** _____

   *What to do when you can't fit into your bathing suit and you leave for vacation in 3 weeks*

9) **Do you** _____ **?**

   *Do you make these common money-draining mistakes when paying your bills every month?*

10) **Discover the** _____ **secrets of** _____

   *Discover the fat burning secrets doctors use when they need to lose weight fast.*

11) **How your** _____ **is ripping you off — and precisely what to do about it (page #)**

   *How your personal trainer is robbing you blind — and exactly what to do about it (page 14)*

12) **A** _____ **method that's helping** _____ **to**

   _____

   *A non-conventional fighting method that's helping skinny weaklings all over the world beat up their former bullies*

13) **Why you need to break all the rules to get**

   _____

   *Why you need to break all the rules you learned as a kid to become a millionaire by the time you're 35*

14) **How to survive your first** _____

   *How to survive your first Tough Mudder race (page #)*

Get instant access to bonus templates,
worksheets, and notes (worth $147) visit
www.WhyDoYouHateMoneyBook.com

# Build Trust And Credibility By Shouldering All The Risk Like A Giant

*"You can have everything you want in life if you will help enough people get what they want."*

— Zig Ziglar

One of the biggest (and hardest) jobs for you will be to remove the fear for your reader, so they are willing to say "yes" because deep down they want you to have the solution to their problems.

The problem is, in today's world, it's hard to believe you're not going to screw them over like everyone else that's said they were going to help them before.

Your job is to think about how you can make yours better than any of your competitors and will increase the likelihood of getting them to buy by knowing you have their best interest at heart.

## Money-Back Guarantees

Besides being legally required to provide a money-back guarantee by credit card processors, there are ways for you to put all the risk on yourself, instead of the reader and slapping on a money back guarantee is a great start.

Yes, it stings when someone takes advantage of the guarantee, and it feels like a personal blow, but if you have a great product and provide your best service, that's all you can do. If you're really selling something that's good, you'll have an extremely low return rate, but it will boost sales like crazy compared to if you don't have one.

There are very few people who buy things just so they can return it (even though it happens on very rare occasions.)

The majority of people just want to solve their problems and know they aren't going to be screwed over.

Here are three different ways to do this, and all of them have different ways you can offer this risk-reversal solution to your new customer: *Free trial, Cheap trial, Money back guarantee.*

The problem is, people have seen money-back-guarantees countless times before which is usually a bad experience. Most everyone I know has tried to cancel a service one time or another, and either had to sit on hold for 45 minutes or jump through hoops of fire over a pit of hot molten magma only to end up having to pay a 50% restocking fee.

An easy way to do this is to increase the length of your

refund policy to 30, 60, 90, or even lifetime guarantees. Some businesses offer to let their customers keep the product even if they ask for a refund.

Here are a few tips for a deal-closing guarantee:

- Write it from a person, not from a company

- Show them you're taking all the risk, not them

- Set the time frame as long as comfortably possible

- Reassure them the process is fast, easy, painless, and stress free

- Clearly state any rules (like they need to show work or show up to 10 sessions)

- Use your guarantee to sell by adding the big benefit, i.e., *"If you don't <u>lose 20 pounds in 6 weeks,</u> I'll give you every penny back"*

When it comes to creating a guarantee, you want to get creative and do everything you can to bear the load of the risk and make it a no-brainer for them.

## Frequently Asked Questions

A "frequently asked question section" is a fantastic place to answer common objections. You want the person reading this to feel like they are the ones asking, so one of the best ways to do this is to take questions you get asked (word for word) and answer them.

- *"How do I know this isn't just another scam?"*

- *"I've tried almost every diet imaginable, what makes [product name different]?"*

- *"What if I try [product name] and it doesn't work? Can I get my money back?"*

You may have already addressed them in the rest of your copy somewhere, but you can do it again here.

## Testimonials & Case Studies

Third party credibility source and examples that agree with what you're saying and prove it to your readers.

Bad testimonials put all the focus on you. Good testimonials focus on the benefit your reader will get.

Here are 3 tips for good testimonials:

1) Talk about a big benefit.
2) Make them about something specific
3) Be as detailed as possible (numbers, examples, etc.)

These are a great way of saying your product or service is the best without having to brag or being worried about selling it too hard… just let your testimonials do their job.

## Premiums And Bonuses

Premium and bonuses are usually offers that don't necessarily directly relate to the main offer, but they increase the perceived value by adding a WOW factor to what you're already offering.

This is a great way to stack on any additional "stuff" that will help your buyer get their results faster, easier, better or simpler.

These extras can be a past product/seminar that's no longer for sale, and this is their only opportunity to get it. If you make your bonuses good enough, some people will buy just for your bonuses.

## Why You Need Urgency AND Scarcity

The BEST offers include both urgency and scarcity.

Urgency and scarcity allow you to frame the consequences for the reader if they don't take action now as a lost opportunity, jump in price, limited quantities, or bonuses disappear, etc.

I shouldn't have to say this but I will… DO NOT lie about these!

If you are closing the cart at a particular time or limiting spaces, actually do it. All it takes is one screw up for you to lose trust and you get thrown into the 'scummy marketer' bucket which is a hard pit to climb out of.

**Urgency:** importance requiring swift action *(i.e., bonuses that go away, deadline for specific price, takeaways)*

**Scarcity:** the state of being scarce or in short supply; shortage *(i.e., limited quantity, limited spots available, limited time open, etc.)*

For example:

"You have only 24 hours left to join my Kickass Copywriting course." This technique uses urgency and has no mention of scarcity.

"The first five people to join my Kickass Copywriting course in the next 24 hours get 1 million high-fives and a 15-second hug from me" combines both urgency (time) and scarcity (limited quantity of 1 million high-fives and hugs.)

Remember, we live in a busy and loud world. If you don't get someone to make a yes or no decision on the spot, the chances of that person coming back and taking action are slim to none.

Give your readers a reason to take action right now. Not later today, tonight, tomorrow or some other time... right now!

## COPY CLIFF NOTES

Different ways to establish trust, credibility, and shoulder all the risk yourself, so your reader turns into a customer.

- **Scarcity:** limited availability
- **Qualify:** accepted by application only
- **Social proof:** join thousands of others
- **Discount for response**: early bird specials
- **Premiums/bonuses**: special offers that expire
- **Limited quantity:** only 100 book copies printed
- **Urgency**: "Only 15 spots available before this group closes"
- **Rules:** you can only buy if you are a women/man/business owner, etc.
- **Takeaways:** bonuses and offers that go away at a specific time or date

Get instant access to bonus templates, worksheets, and notes (worth $147) visit www.WhyDoYouHateMoneyBook.com

# The Keys To Crafting An Irresistible Offer Which Make Buying A No-Brainer

*"Copy is not written. If anyone tells you 'you write copy', sneer at them. Copy is not written. Copy is assembled. You do not write copy, you assemble it. You are working with a series of building blocks, you are putting the building blocks together, and then you are putting them in certain structures, you are building a little city of desire for your person to come and live in."*

— Eugene Schwartz

The best copy in the world will not make up for a weak offer, but 'a strong offer' will give you more leeway for 'not-so-great copy.'

And let's be honest here, if you're reading this book, you don't have plans on being the best damn copywriter on the face of this planet.

If you did everything, you were supposed to up until now, most of the selling is done for you. Your offer is when your prospect realizes they need what you're selling and you give them the next steps.

Your job is to create an irresistible package for your prospect that's so good they can't refuse it. This isn't just the product, and it's price – It's the features and benefits, bonuses, guarantee, urgency, scarcity, and finally the cost... that's what makes a good offer so irresistible.

## Look Deeper Than Your Direct Competitors

Start by taking a look at what your competitors are offering and what they are doing. Now all you have to do is create something better – and I don't mean by lowering the price.

Remember, people are not buying your product or service, they're buying for the solution and who it lets them become, so I want you to think outside the box.

Let's say you're an in-home trainer who primarily works with corporate executives who want to lose their gut and drop their blood pressure because the doctor told them they're on the fast track to a heart attack if something doesn't change fast.

Most trainers look for other trainers who work with this type of client. Sure, these people are competitors, but they're not your only competitors. Think about it, personal training is just ONE small way they're looking to solve their problem.

What about prescription medications, juice cleanses, supplements, shake diets, boot camps classes, running club, spin classes, medical procedures, and everything else they're looking at before hiring a personal trainer?

Don't just look at products which help solve the surface issue, look at every possible option your reader could look for to solve their problem. When you do this, you can showcase why your offer is better than these alternatives and craft a compelling and genuinely irresistible offer.

Remember, an irresistible offer is apparent, specific, and tells your prospect precisely what to do next. The more you can describe the outcome and what your reader will do and who they become in the future, the better.

They need to know exactly what to do, how to do it, when to do it, and what's going to happen next.

## Restate And Eliminate Objections

Instead of looking at buyer objections as resistance, look at objections to questions that weren't answered yet.

This means someone is showing interest in what you have, as opposed to just closing the tab or immediately tuning you out. I had a hard time figuring this out because I used to feel like they were trying to back me into the corner when in reality, this displays their interest.

A good place to start is to list every reason possible reason someone won't buy so you can address any fear, doubt, and excuse they might use.

It's too cheap

It's too expensive

I don't want the hassle

It sounds too good to be true

I'm afraid of getting ripped off

I'm afraid of feeling foolish if I do get ripped off

I don't want people making fun of me for trying this

. . . and so on.

This is where knowing your audience is key, because not only do you know what they want but you know what scares them and what they don't want. Now, you can turn your disadvantages into advantages and use a few of these secrets to smash price objections and show the value of your product.

Price objections are one of the most common sales objections you're going to face when selling anything. People want to know why what you're selling costs what it does. They aren't saying it's right or wrong, but it's your job to explain to them why the price is justified and why it's a great offer for them.

Here are a few ways to do that:

## #1. Compare Apples to Oranges – Not Apples to Apples

I first learned about the concept of comparing apples to oranges from master marketer Todd Brown of Marketing Funnel Automation.

Todd explains "The apple is buying DVDs and watching them at home. The orange is booking your hotel, paying for hotel food, potentially purchasing plane tickets (or at least paying for gas and parking), being away from your family, being away from your business, and traveling alone. All of that, without even including the price of the event itself, will cost you several thousand dollars. On the other hand, you can get the entire set of DVDs, all the education, all the speakers, all the answers and materials, for a mere fraction of attending live."

Can you see how powerful that is?

You're the best option, not because you're offering the lowest price but because you know what you're doing and will solve their biggest problem.

If you're selling an ebook, the last thing you want to do is compare your ebook to other ebooks. Instead, compare it to the cost the reader would have if they had to fly across the country to attend a 1:1 seminar with you, what they would pay for lodging, food, transportation, time away from work, etc.

Now they can learn from the comfort of their own home and still get paid to do it.

## #2. Price Stack For a WOW Factor

This is a way to exponentially explode the value of what you're selling to make it an easy decision. Don't just pull a part of the original program or service out and call it a bonus… especially if it's needed to all work together.

They have to see value in your bonus. In fact, some people will even buy just for the bonus' — that's how you know you did it right. Think of things like never seen before interviews, special reports, discontinued products, etc.

Price stacking can add even more value to the product or be something very different that can still help.

## #3. What This Solution Costs You

What would it cost them if they went about getting the same information the way that you did?

You can also discuss everything that went into the development… time, years in college, $ spent on courses, travel, and blood sweat and tears.

## #4. Show Them Their Future

One way to beat price objections is to show the reader what they're life will probably be like if they don't buy the product... *Will they continue down the same path? Will it get worse? Will it get better?*

Painting the picture of the future, good or bad, can be a powerful way to close the deal.

## Ask For The Sale... Dun Dun Dun Dun

Yes, I know, this is probably the hardest part for you. But the good part is, you're not face-to-face with the person, so it makes it so much easier.

And honestly, it's the hard part for pretty much everyone, at least at some point in their lives.

The thing is, you already did all of the hard work, and now all you have to do is present the offer to someone who is happy to exchange some dollars for a result they want.

The most common mistake you can make is never asking for the sale, which means there's a very high chance you're not going to get it. But if you offer someone a solution to a huge problem they're having and tell them what they have to do to get that solution they're most likely going to do it.

I understand the weird feeling about asking for money, but you're not there in person for the rejection, so what does it matter?

That's why selling with words (like you're learning in this book) is a great tool and will skyrocket your in-person selling abilities too. What you need to realize is your only job is to elicit a clear decision.

"Yes" is a great answer to hear and "No" isn't a great response but it's not bad either… because at least you have done your job to get a response.

In a second I am going to outline an easy template for you to use when creating your offer but first make sure you went through the Mind-Reading phase.

If you did your prospect research, you know who you're talking to, what their #1 problem is, and what is holding them back from buying and so much more.

Once you have that, answer these questions to help you craft an irresistible offer:

1) *Name and simple description of what you're offering?*

2) *What is the primary promise (solves #1 biggest problem)?*

3) *What are 3-5 secondary promises (solve secondary problems)?*

4) *What are the key features and benefits of those features?*

5) *What is your guarantee and bonuses?*

6) *How is it different than your competitors?*

After you have the answers to these questions, you have everything you need to put the perfect offer together.

## COPY CLIFF NOTES

Obviously, for short copy pages, some of these might not be included, but you can do your best to combine and touch on as many points as you can.

The more of these elements you can offer the better:

- **Product name and who it's for**
- **#1 biggest problem it will solve**
- **Establish value:** *3-5 secondary promises*
- **What you get:** *specific deliverables with features/benefits*
- **Bonuses**: adds value and make it a no-brainer
- **Price:** sell them the outcome of the product and price is almost meaningless
- **Trivialize Price:** *compare apples to oranges*
- **Guarantee**: take away risk
- **Why they need to act now:** *scarcity and urgency*
- **What to do next:** *exact steps*

When you combine the elements of an irresistible offer with the risk-reversal techniques from the last chapter, you've got yourself one hell of a deal!

Get instant access to bonus templates, worksheets, and notes (worth $147) visit www.WhyDoYouHateMoneyBook.com

# How To Quickly Write A Sales Message That Converts

*"Let us prove to the world that good taste, good art, and good writing can be good selling."*
— William Bernbach

Putting together your own sales page could be an entire book itself, so I just want to cover the basics of setting up a high converting sales page that: can be used to sell your coaching services, products, books, courses, challenges, etc.

Make sure to have your customer research at your side while you're writing your sales page. In fact, you can even cut and paste answers and responses from your research into your copy.

Whatever you do, DO NOT start writing your sales page until after you've done your customer and market research.

The first step is to outline the page. We already did most of the work, so this part should be easy

Here are two popular and simple sales page templates for you to start with:

Headline
Intro/Hook/Story
Bullets
Offer** (start here)
Risk Reversal
Close

Headline
Intro
Hook/Story
Offer** (start here)
Bullets
Value Add (bonuses)
Guarantee
Takeaway/Scarcity
Close
P.S.
Order

As you can probably see by the **, the templates are telling you to start with the offer.

I know it sounds weird, but remember the offer is one of the most crucial parts of your copy, so you want to make sure it's dialed in which is why I dedicated the previous chapter to it (and pretty much the one before too.)

After you write the general outline for your page, then "write an offer so good they can't refuse."

An offer so good it would make Don Corleone proud, then it's time to write your big idea/hook.

Then write at least 20 headlines, 20 bullets, and fill in the rest of your first draft.

This isn't the only way to do things, but this is what I found to work best for me and is the quickest. One other option is to start by writing the offer and then lists of bullets and then getting into the rest of the page.

What I don't suggest doing is just starting from the top and randomly making your way around. You're going to spend so much time writing, deleting, editing and doing things that you didn't have to do in the first place.

Now that you have the basics of a sales page written, here are some pro tips for you:

## 13 Persuasive Tips Everyone Ought To Know When Writing Sales Copy

1) **Quote People:** Quotes are a fantastic way to show how you can help people just like your reader to get XYZ result of their dreams. Quotes give them social proof, builds trust, and allows them to see it's possible for them.

2) **Emotionally Connect With Them:** You can emotionally connect with your readers by appealing to them, but first, you must understand who they are and what they want. This is why the Mind Reading phase is critical.

3) **Make Them Feel A Part of Something Bigger:** Do anything you can to make the person reading your message feel a part of something special. Community, bigger purpose, movement, club, a group of people just like them who all want the same thing they do.

4) **Twist The Knife:** We all know things might be bad now but digging into the real pain behind why they are feeling what they are feeling and what they want to do about it is massive. Bringing this harsh reality to the table is something that many people are afraid to do, but it often needs to be said because it's the truth.

5) **Tell Amazing Stories:** The most memorable way to cement something in someone's brain is to tell a story or teach something that is easily relatable. You don't have to be a storytelling master… just think setup, plot, and a punchline and refer back to the storytelling chapter to get the basics down.

6) **Use Metaphors and Analogies:** These are a shortcut to painting vivid pictures in your reader's mind by appealing to different learning senses. Saying "Being an accountant was a cancer to my dreams' is much more powerful than "I was an accountant before a personal trainer."

7) **Use Rhetorical Questions:** Sounds silly to ask questions in your writing, doesn't it? Well, when the answer is obvious, these rhetorical questions add a strong emotional punch to your writing and makes your reader feel like they're having a conversation with you.

8) **Show The Path Of Possibilities**: Tease, tempt, and be the crystal ball for the person reading your message. How amazing could their life be if they say yes? Who and what do they become? What are the doors that open when they become this person? By giving examples of possibilities, you allow them to paint the picture for themselves.

9) **The Consequences Of Your Decision:** What will their life be like if they say "No", especially if their life is bad now? What do they lose? What's going to happen if they keep going down the same path? Are they going to stay the same or get worse?

10) **Create An Us vs. Them Mentality:** Humans are tribal, it's in our DNA, and there's just no getting around it. By establishing a Us vs. Them mentality, you're creating a unified stand against all the other bullshit they've tried in the past and failed. If you can show how you're different, and you hate those failures just as much as they do, you're going to gain a fan. Everyone likes to be on the side of people who are already throwing rocks at their enemies.

11) **Confirm Their Suspicions:** Don't hide their suspicions. Do everything you can to air them out and answer them with complete honesty. Address objections, doubts, and fears that can hold your prospect back from taking action. A great way to do this is with Q & A's, testimonials, stories, etc.

12) **Let Them Know THEY Can Decide:** Make it clear that THEY are the ones that get to decide and have complete control over their decision. If you've laid everything out correctly, this is everything that they want, but they don't want to feel pressured into something.

13) **Elicit A Clear Answer:** "Yes or no." that's it. Maybe's are no's. They already know the possibilities of both outcomes because you've laid it out for them, so tell them exactly what to do next, be sure they make a clear "yes" or "no" decision.

If you can nail these 13 persuasive tips you've got yourself a kickass sales message. Congrats.

## COPY CLIFF NOTES

Step #1: Outline your sales page.

Step #2: Start with your offer

Step #3: Come up with your big idea/hook

Step #4: Write at least 20+ headlines

Step #5: Write at least 20+ bullets

Step #6: Fill in the rest for your first draft

Be sure to keep an eye on the 13 tips above when reviewing your sales page. The more of these you can include, the more successful your message will be.

Get instant access to bonus templates, worksheets, and notes (worth $147) visit www.WhyDoYouHateMoneyBook.com

# Write Cash-Generating Emails Like A Million Dollar Copywriter... Without Actually Being One

*"What really knocks me out is a book that, when you're all done reading it, you wish the author that wrote it was a terrific friend of yours and you could call him up on the phone whenever you felt like it."*

— J.D. Salinger

… That's the feeling you want to create with your emails.

Plummeting open rates, messages landing in the junk folder, unanswered questions, declining open rates, and so much more.

But is email marketing is dead? It's happening for some, but not for all.

Did you know that in 2008 the Obama campaign raised over 10 million dollars from a single email?

If you can learn how to write good emails, it's FAR from being dead.

Email holds more attention and intimacy than social media and is still the primary delivery source for IMPORTANT information.

Think about it, when you order something from Amazon do they send your receipt to your social media inbox or do they send it via email? What about when you go to the doctor's office?

That's right, email. Email reigns king for sales.

Not to mention once you have email marketing down, it's easily scalable to ridiculously large numbers of people. The key is to get someone to give you their primary email address and not the email address they use to sign up for stuff and never check.

On top of that, if anything ever happens, you still have access to that list. In simple terms, Facebook and Instagram are also lists, but if they decide to change their policies, disappear, or become irrelevant like Myspace, you're out of luck. Same goes for getting banned or blacklisted on an advertising platform like Google Adwords or Facebook. But with an email list, you still have that same list no matter what.

According to Fortune magazine, the average adult receives 147 emails every single day, so it's your job to stand out. This also means you can't just go spamming people's inboxes. You have to learn how to write emails that people want to read.

**Your #1 Goal For Email Marketing:** Create a bond close enough that your readers anxiously anticipate your emails because you are sharing valuable and entertaining information with them.

You see, the people who are most engaged in what you have to say, interested in you and your company, are the ones that are going to take action.

There are two basic types of emails: daily emails and launch-campaign emails. To keep things from getting too complicated, I'll show you seven launch campaigns then focus on daily emails.

# 7 Basic Email Launch Campaigns

There are thousands of different things you can be doing with email campaigns that most businesses never even thought about, and that's a beauty of it. But I don't want you to get overwhelmed.

Once you get the basics down of these seven launch campaigns, you will see the endless possibilities in your business and how you can add to current funnels, create new ones, add effective follow-ups and ascend clients through your business to ultimately give them precisely what they want and need.

> **Welcome campaign:** an email or series of emails to welcome new subscribers and familiarize them with you and speed up the relationship building process.

**Product launch campaign:** a well thought out series of emails that brings customers through a controlled buying process for a specific product or service. When you get to the sales email, use the simple template I gave you in the sales page section as an outline: subject line, intro, hook, offer, call to action, close, p.s. with another call to action.

**Coaching campaign:** when someone buys a product or service, you want them to use the product or service immediately. This reminds the reader that they've made a smart choice and will prevent buyer's remorse while also thanking them for being a kickass customer.

**Non-buyer campaign:** Use this to find out why someone didn't buy and follow up with an offer to better suit their needs. You can use this data to improve your offer and is either done with an email reply or a survey to fill out to keep responses in order.

**Ascension campaign:** offer up-sells, cross-sells and other additional benefits for new buyers that can help speed up the results they're after or that compliment what they've purchased like added accountability or access.

**Re-engagement campaign:** bring back to life unengaged subscribers who you haven't heard from in a while or when cooking up a new and different offer. Keep these emails short and get creative with the subject lines to catch attention.

**Segmentation campaign**: tag and move subscribers into 'buckets' so you can provide targeted offers that best suit their interests instead of blasting them with things they don't hold their attention.

These should give you a much better idea of the different types of campaigns you can implement in your business today or in the future.

And when you take a look at the sales funnel chapters you'll get a much better understanding of the process and possibilities you can map out with this.

Almost every client I write emails for finds easy money by adding one or more of these email campaigns into their business which has the potential to generate money over and over again.

… Onward, to daily emails…

## Daily Emails

Daily emails kick-ass.

They're frequently sent emails, hence the word "daily" but doesn't necessarily mean you MUST send them every single day. By sending these 'one-off' emails, you're able to engage your audience, build a closer connection, and stay relevant by using infotainment.

The emails used are typically story-based lessons that add value to your reader's life in some way, shape, or form. It can be a laugh, a helpful nugget, a spark of inspiration, a fun task, or a tip that's going to bust them through a barrier.

Frequent emailing is one of the best ways to build love, trust, and authority — it's not a 24/7 pitch fest.

If you do it right, you'll get messages from people saying things like "I look forward to reading your emails every day." or "Hey, I missed your email yesterday, is everything ok?" if you skip out on a day.

These types of emails are 'one-off' stories like episodes of South Park or Seinfeld so your reader doesn't necessarily have to see your previous email to understand what is going on, compared to some of the launch campaigns which can tell stories over a few emails. Both of those TV shows can help you become a better writer and storyteller and a bank of unlimited ideas.

This book already has ideas for how to destroy writer's block, but I want you to start thinking about your life as a movie, and anything that happens can be used to teach a lesson or to help one of your readers.

Check out the 'Copy Cliff Notes' for 13 plug-and-play emails ideas.

If you're not sure where to start, follow AIDA… a simple formula that can be used to create impressive emails without a problem:

Attention

Interest

Desire

Action

… You'll notice how some of these can overlap like the attention and interest, or interest and desire. Just imagine if your subject line and email contain all of these.

For a brilliant display of daily/frequent emails check out Ben Settle, Ryan Lee, Doberman Dan, and John Carlton. I've learned a boatload about each of them. But be warned… you're going to end up buying something.

## COPY CLIFF NOTES

Remember, your #1 goal when writing emails are to create a relationship where your readers love that part of their day when they read what you have to say.

Effective email marketing uses a combination of email launch campaigns and daily engagement emails. But, if you're starting from scratch, write a welcome series. Keep it very simple at first.

Give them the reason they joined (free-gift), introduce yourself, let them know why that's important to them and how you can help them, and ask for a reply.

Not only does this cover the bare basics, but getting a reply early on initiates a two-way conversation right from the start and tells their email provider you're a person they want to have an interview with, not a spammer.

Here are 13 plug-and-play email ideas that you can run with:

1) Movie plots

2) Movie quotes

3) Movie characters

4) Your darkest secret

5) Client question/story

6) Myths about your niche

7) A commonly asked question

8) A quick win for you or a client

9) Get a response by asking a question

10) Common mistakes your avatar makes

11) Most embarrassing moment of your life

12) A discovery that changed how you look at something

13) All current events *(elections, celebrity shenanigans, holidays, etc)*

As you can see, this is just the tip of the iceberg.

Each of these have an unlimited number of ways for you to spin it, and you can have kickass emails forever.

Get instant access to bonus templates,
worksheets, and notes (worth $147) visit
www.WhyDoYouHateMoneyBook.com

# The 10 Commandments Of Writing Kickass Emails

*"You get ideas from daydreaming. You get ideas from being bored. You get ideas all the time. The only difference between writers and other people is we notice when we're doing it."*

— Neil Gaiman

## #1. Make It About Your Reader (Not You)

The most important commandment of all. The person reading your email doesn't care about you, they care about themselves which is why they open every email thinking "what's in it for me?" Your job is to help them solve their problem or provide them with value in some way, i.e., a lesson, tool, hack, laugh, etc.

## #2. Only Send Emails To People Who Have Asked

Do NOT send emails to people unless they have permitted you. Not only is it annoying but it's illegal. On top of that, you can get peppered with SPAM complaints which can negatively influence your deliverability rate in the future, which means email providers like Gmail are way more likely to send your messages to the junk folder.

## #3. Put Time Into Your Subject Line (and Sender Name)

If you write terrific emails that never get opened, what's the point? Which is precisely why it's so critical to put time, energy, and focus on writing a good subject line that will entice your reader to open the email and see what's inside. It's the start of the slippery slope. Some of the best email subject lines follow the [curiosity + benefit] formula. Make sure you're 'from name' is something personal that your reader will recognize and not skip over. Ian Stanley uses off the wall sender names and subject lines brilliantly.

## #4. Use Infotainment

I first learned about 'infotainment' from the evil genius and email marketing master Mr. Ben Settle, who is known for his daily emails. Infotainment is the concept of creating content that includes a mixture of information and entertainment. Ben recommends 80% entertainment and 20% educational content. The actual ratio will depend on how great of a writer and communicator you are but the moral of the story is, don't be boring. Use stories to teach, engage, interact, and sell because people buy on emotion, not logic. Your goal should be for your emails to have a personality that people are dying to read.

## #5. Build As Much Trust As Possible

Show up consistently and show empathy. It's much easier to trust someone when they know you have their best interest at heart. Once you understand their needs, wants, desires, and struggles, you will develop raving fans and the best way to figure that out is by showing up consistently. My good friend Mike Vacanti built a very successful fitness by caring a ton and putting out killer content non-stop even when people weren't watching.

## #6. Write To One-person

You want your writing to feel like you're sitting on the edge of your chair in an engaging conversation with ONE person, not a stadium full of people. If you need to, write a person's name at the top of the email and start it as a personal letter, then when you're editing go back and delete that part.

## #7. Write How You Speak

I don't mean put a bunch of um's and ah's in there. Make your writing sound like a conversation. This is where transitional phrases, writing rhythm and using words like you and your reader use in real life conversations are especially important.

## #8. Hit "SEND" Consistently

The last thing you want to do is wait weeks or months to mail your list and when you send them something they forget who you are. If you followed commandment #2, they raised their hand so now it's your job to build the relationship with consistency. Most lists do best with 3-5 emails per week. At a minimum send one email per week, so people don't forget about you. Build a relationship:

## #9. Have One Clear Goal And Sell "The Click"

Every email you write you should have ONE goal for the reader to take (i.e., watch this video, leave a comment, reply, learn more, etc.) You can still use more than one call to action link in the email but they should all focus on the same action. Keep in mind, your job in email is to sell the act of clicking the link, not what's on the other side of the action. So if you're selling a product and the link directs them to the sales page, get them to click through and let the sales page do its job.

## #10. Avoid SPAM words

The fastest way to land in the junk folder is to use words that trigger email providers to register your email as junk, especially in your subject line. Think along the lines of FREE, cancel anytime, 100% free, join millions, SPAM… Google "Email Spam Triggers" to get a better idea of what words to avoid in your emails.

## COPY CLIFF NOTES

If you follow these ten email commandments, you'll be writing kickass emails that people love to read in no time.

1) Make It About Your Reader (Not You)

2) Only Send Emails To People Who Have Asked

3) Put Time Into Your Subject Line (and Sender Name)

4) Use Infotainment

5) Build As Much Trust As Possible

6) Write To One-person

7) Write How You Speak

8) Hit "SEND" Consistently

9) Have One Clear Goal And Sell "The Click"

10) Avoid SPAM words

# Simple And Effective Editing Tricks For A Seamless Read

*"It is perfectly okay to write garbage —
as long as you edit brilliantly."*

— C. J. Cherryh

Now that you've learned all the in's and out's about writing great copy that hits home with your audience, we have to make sure it's easy to read otherwise all that hard works go to waste.

If you're like me, you weren't blessed with the gift of writing beautiful words at the drop of a hat. Instead, I had to learn what goes into writing well and I had to practice and edit my ass off to make it sound good.

This chapter will focus on a few writing and editing hacks I use that will make writing more comfortable, as well as, being more enjoyable and convincing.

The first step is to brain dump and vomit your words all over the page. Do this with as little editing, fixing, and backspacing as possible. If you do this right, it's the quickest part of the writing process.

The magic lies in the editing.

The editing is where we make the copy easy to read as well as exciting and beneficial. I recommend using an editor like 'Grammarly' to check for spelling errors. If you really suck at sentence structure, they will give you some recommendations.

"The Hemingway app" can be a good start too, but don't take their recommendations as gospel. It can make your writing very dry if you follow everything to a "T." One of the most significant benefits of using The Hemingway App is the readability function. As a general rule of thumb, you want to get the reading level down to about 5th grade or so (depending on your audience), so it's easy to read for all levels.

Now, onto the fun stuff. In this section, we're going to cover the basics of editing for easy to read copy.

## Edit In Full Passes

Make sure you edit your work in full passes.

Most people make the mistake of editing a few paragraphs, returning to the top, editing a few again, returning to the top and repeating over and over again. When they're finished, the beginning was edited over 10+ times, but the end was edited once or twice.

What you want to do is edit in full passes, meaning ALL of the writing at once. Then you can repeat and do it again.

## Read It Out Loud

Reading your writing out loud is the single best way to improve your copy and should be step 1,2,3, and 4, but the truth is many people will skip this anyway.

That's worth repeating:

"The best way to improve your writing is to read it out loud."

You should always ruthlessly judge what you're writing by paying attention to a few things:

> Does your copy flow?
>
> Is your message clear?
>
> Does it spark emotions?
>
> Will your reader connect with it?
>
> Do they know what to do next?

You can read through your writing over and over again and still miss spelling errors and think sentences sound good but when you read it out loud, you'll stumble over words like there's no tomorrow.

When you write, you have an idea of how you want it to sound and how you want it to come across, but that doesn't mean it's written that way.

The best way to find out is to read it out loud.

When you find sentences that make you stumble over words or are hard to read, rearrange until the words roll off the tongue.

## Have Someone Else Read Your Writing

Again, a lot of people will skip this one for many different reasons. Mostly because they read it out loud themselves or are afraid of getting feedback that won't be sunshine and rainbows.

Having someone else read your copy will help find even more loose ends, BUT is even MORE beneficial. Here's why:

You're looking for things which are: confusing, places they lose attention, words that don't make sense, jargon that flies over their head, and most importantly how they feel after!

If they say "I liked it" or "Your writing is good," that's a bad sign. You've got some work to do. Instead, what you want is for them to take whatever action you were writing about.

Was it to buy? Great, they should be asking you how they can buy it.

# Remove Qualifiers That Rob Your Writing Of Certainty

Grammarly.com defines a qualifier as:

"A word that limits or enhances another word's meaning. Qualifiers affect the certainty and specificity of a statement. Overusing certain types of qualifiers (for example, very or really) can make a piece of writing sound lazily constructed."

In our case, we are removing qualifiers that take away the power and certainty from your writing and suck the energy out of any claims you make.

For example, which sounds more powerful to you" "This diet might work" or "I guarantee this diet WILL do XYZ."

Common qualifiers you want to remove end in 'ly.'

Here's a short list of typical words you're going to want to remove wherever possible. :

| | |
|---|---|
| *like* | *may* |
| *might* | *some* |
| *hardly* | *could* |
| *usually* | *mostly* |
| *generally* | *partially* |
| *possibly* | *basically* |

Don't stress about these when you're writing. The editing process is when you are going to clean this up.

## Add Power, Emotion, And Clarity By Using Better Words

All words have meaning and emotion tied to them which we use to paint pictures in our minds.

If I said something about the old guy I see in the morning, that wouldn't do much for you. It's boring, bland, and not descriptive. You have no idea who, what, or where I used to see him.

What's this old geezer doing? Did he smell like an old dude? What did he dress like?

The picture you paint sucks. What if I approached it like this...

"He's talking about Big Tim.. the jacked old guy I see every morning throwing weights around like they're peanuts. This dude looks like a shredded Santa and squats 500 so easy it's like he's sitting down in a chair." That paints an entirely different picture in your mind.

The number one rule for writing is never to bore your reader. Otherwise, they're going to leave. Using power words is a surefire way make sure that doesn't happen.

Power words paint a picture and come with extra emotion

and feelings attached to them. They add the extra "umph" to your writing.

You can use power words to add shock value, convey an action, or catch your reader's attention with a clever phrase.

*Mad* => **livid**

*Eat* => **feast**

*Kill* => **slaughter**

*Tricky* => **Voodoo**

*Beat* => **dominate**

*Quiet* => **secretive**

*Scary* => **intimidating**

*Loud* => **bone crunching**

*Rare* => **impossible to find**

*Bad idea* => **career suicide**

*Interested* => **dying to know**

*Hidden* => **cleverly disguised**

*Tried hard* => **bend over backwards**

Each writer will have a go-to arsenal of power words, and each market will identify with certain words as well.

Highlight or write down your favorite power words as you read and go through your day-to-day life. Refer back to them before you write, but more importantly, review your power words when you are editing. Then swap out boring and meaningless words for jaw-dropping, heart-pounding, knee-shaking ones.

For more examples, google "power words' and get the book "Words That Sell" by Richard Bayan.

## COPY CLIFF NOTES

Now that you've word vomited all the junk in your brain into one place, you're going to turn these words into a beautifully written piece of gold by following these simple (yet effective) editing tips:

- Edit in full passes
- Read your writing out loud
- Have someone else read your writing
- Remove qualifiers
- Add Power words

Once you've done this, you can use the tricks found in the next chapter to boost your writing to from good to great.

Get instant access to bonus templates,
worksheets, and notes (worth $147) visit
www.WhyDoYouHateMoneyBook.com

# Three Little-Known Editing Cheat Codes To Take Your Writing From Good To Great

*"Not a wasted word. This has been main point to my literary thinking all my life"*

— Hunter S. Thompson

When we get down to the nitty-gritty, copywriting is just a means to transport a message from one brain to another.

But you can always tell when someone is trying to be too cute and "spice things up" with poet-like sentence structure that the average person stumbles on and is difficult to read.

Instead of bombing out and hearing crickets, make sure your words flow effortlessly.

No breaks, No stumbles. Just short, punchy, smooth sentences that roll off the tongue.

You see, great copy does a few fundamental things.

It gets the person reading it to nod their head, drop their guard, and say "Wow, he gets me." It pushes emotional buttons. It creates an itch that must be scratched, and YOU happen to have the PERFECT back scratcher.

This is why you want your message to be clear, not cute. No big words and no confusion.

To this day I have yet to hear someone say "Man, this is perfect for me, and I'd love it, but I just don't think it's complicated enough for me so I can't buy it."

Most of these advanced editing hacks I first discovered from Bond Halbert's book "The Halbert Copywriting Method Part III." It's a fantastic read and he brings you step by step through the editing process which is one of the most important pieces.

## Emphasize Words And Use Punctuation To Change How Your Copy Is Read

What you meant to write and what you write aren't always the same.

If you've read your writing out loud, you'll understand what I mean. You'll find words that don't make sense, places where you stumble and struggle to get the words out, and pieces that just don't sound "right."

There is a certain rhythm to writing copy, and that beat is lost when you skip editing and reading your text out loud. Your job as a writer is to make what you write crystal clear to your readers, and you can do this by emphasizing certain words and using punctuation.

Here are a few ways you can use punctuation to change how your writing is read:

Font

**Bold**

CAPS

*Italics*

Colors

**Size**

"Quotes"

Highlight

Underline

!?%* Punctuation !?%*

## Provide Eye Relief And Easy Reading

If the primary goal is to get someone to slide down the slippery slope you've created with your writing; you need to provide eye relief.

This is what's known as readability, which is basically how easy it is to read something. There are a lot of different factors that go into this such as font type, size, color, line spacing, paragraph spacing, and more.

Do you notice how the paragraphs in this book are different from the ones your teacher taught you how to write in school?

They are short, punchy, and to the point. This creates a rhythmic flow to reading and is less intimidating than looking at a full page of block text.

There are a lot of things which affect readability we're going to look at three easy ones:

**Fonts:** Online use 'Sans-Serif' fonts like Verdana, Arial, Lato, Helvetica but for hard copy print use 'Serif' fonts like Times New Roman, Georgia, and Bakersville,

**Paragraphs**: Keep sentences short. No more than 3-5 lines a section.

**Break up your copy**: Videos, charts, graphs, Photos, Subheads, Infographics, Numbers (1,2,3), Simulate Handwriting, Infographics, etc.

# Use Transitional Phrases and Cliff Hangers

These are a surefire way to keep your reader sliding down the slippery slope.

Ending sentences with questions is a great way to keep attention as well as adding transitional phrases like these:

| | |
|---|---|
| *So* | *Yet* |
| *Suddenly* | *The result?* |
| *Want proof?* | *Now, tell me…* |
| *But there's more* | *Let me explain…* |
| *Can this be true?* | *Things got worse* |
| *There's a saying…* | *Here's the real kicker* |
| *But what if you could…* | *How can you beat that?* |
| *Ok, I'm nearly done, but…* | *That's not even the best part…* |
| *What does this all mean to you?* | *Then came the real shocking part* |

Google "117 transitional phrases" and you can print out a sheet to refer back to when you edit your writing.

## COPY CLIFF NOTES

1) Use punctuation to emphasize how your writing is read

2) Be aware of font types, sizes, paragraph spaces, paragraph length, and adding elements to break up your copy

3) Use transitional words and phrases, so your writing feels like a conversation, not a public service announcement.

For a full guide to editing get your hands on a copy of 'The Halbert Copywriting Method Part III' by Bond Halbert.

Get instant access to bonus templates, worksheets, and notes (worth $147) visit www.WhyDoYouHateMoneyBook.com

# How To Cure Writer's Block Once and For All

*"People on the outside think there's something magical about writing, that you go up in the attic at midnight and cast the bones and come down in the morning with a story. But it isn't like that. You sit in back of the typewriter and you work, and that's all there is to it."*

— Harlan Ellison

For most writers, this chapter is worth 100x the investment you made in this book.

Many people will tell you "writer's block" is one of the most agonizing, self-defeating, and painful experiences in life.

Personally, I think the excuse of staring at a blank screen and blinking cursor and blaming writer's block is a way to drown in self-pity. It is a terrible excuse and a complete load of horse shit.

It's just an excuse. There's no doubt in my mind that people who struggle with writer's block go into writing with the intention of creating a masterpiece on the first go and will fight until the sun comes up.

Now I'm far from being the best writer in the world, but when I write copy, I rarely struggle with writer's block. This isn't because of some mutant writing gene or a magic pill. It's quite simple.

I just write. Because I honestly don't see any good that can come out of staring at a blank screen while I tell myself I have no idea what to write. It's annoying, frustrating, and discouraging.

Here's how to get over that initial hump.

# 3.5 Ways To Fight Off Writer's Block And Spit Out Epic Content

## #1. Write a fact

It could be something you're looking at in the room, your favorite movie quotes, a plot of a story, the incredible feeling a new pair of socks feels on your feet, etc.

Staring a blank page is intimidating, so it's important to get something down on the page then continue adding words to the page.

## #2. Write 3-5 main points

Write down a few points you want to make, ideas you have, statements you'd like to share, or questions you'd like answered.

These points will serve as an outline and prompt for you to start writing. Don't overthink this. These can stay as overarching themes in your content, or they can be taken out when things start to flow.

## #3. Word vomit

Just spit it out and stop agonizing over every keystroke in your first draft. If you want to torment yourself, do it when you're editing because that's when it matters.

Now is the time to sit down and drop everything into the first draft with as little editing, formatting, backspacing, deleting, and reworking as possible.

It's hard, It's painful, It's easier said than done, and I still struggle with this. I find myself tagging the backspace button like it's my best friend, editing as I go, and formatting line by line but it slows me down and breaks up my flow.

I got a good tip from Founder and CEO of ConvertKit, Nathan Barry, to help with this.

… Put a piece of tape over your backspace key so you literally can't use it!

## #3.5. Stop and Start

This will ultimately change the game if you can follow this one.

> STOP: wasting all your time sucking in more information
>
> START: creating killer content that helps people

A key thing to remember is, the first words you're putting on the page don't even have to be the right words because you are going to come back and edit later. The action is the most critical part.

It's like going to the gym when you don't want to. When everything in your life is telling you not to go, you're tired, you need a break, and you're better off just sitting at home. But you go anyway and have one of the most amazing workouts ever.

That's the hurdle that most people have to get over with writing, so don't just stare at a blank screen and get pissed off at yourself.

## COPY CLIFF NOTES

- Write a fact (any fact)
- Write 3-5 main points to serve as an outline
- Word vomit onto the page
- Stop analyzing and start taking action

Get instant access to bonus templates,
worksheets, and notes (worth $147) visit
www.WhyDoYouHateMoneyBook.com

# 13 Ways To Spark Writing Inspiration And Get The Juices Flowing

*"You can't wait for inspiration.*
*You have to go after it with a club"*

— Jack London

## Juggle

Bet you didn't see this one coming. You think I'm kidding, don't you? I'm not. If you don't know how to juggle, you can learn easily. I taught myself how to do it within a day while writing this book and working on client projects. Learning a skill like this helps train your vision, coordination, touch and many other things that often go untrained. Not only is it fun, but this can drastically improve your creativity and writing.

## Read Fiction

Reading fiction is a great way to get your creative juices flowing and give you ideas. If you have trouble writing, I highly suggest you pick up a few fiction books to read or listen to when you are going about your day. I recommend checking out Lee Child, Stephen King, J.K. Rowling.

## Exercise

If you're not doing this already, you're missing out on a whole lot of productivity and creativity. Your body is the fastest gateway to clarity, strength, and power — both mentally and physically. When you take care of your body, you also strengthen your mind. If you're stuck in a rut, go workout and clear your head. A lot of writers claim brilliant ideas and hooks are found during long runs, bikes rides, and hikes. Hell, you can even lunge around town. In fact, the first time I was talked to Jay Ferruggia on the phone I was lunging down the street to the gym to get some creative juices flowing.

## Brain Drugs

Adding cognitive enhancers like coffee and nootropics help non-writers focus a lot. Just be careful not to overstimulate with caffeine so that you're so jittery your hands start going crazy, or you feel like you're going to throw up. I learned this the hard way plenty of times.

## Write Facts

The act of staring at a blank screen is what scares people, so this is simple. Not only does it take that away but it gets you used to punch keys, and the act of writing has begun. Start by writing FACTS: name, date, outline the piece, a sentence that is true like the weather or something about a friend, just blabber on about nothing, etc.

## Take a Siesta

Take 5 minutes before you sit down to write to clear your head and get focused. If you don't meditate (aka take a siesta) now, I highly suggest you start picking up the habit… it's a game changer. I'm not telling you, you have to rub crystals on your nipples or do anything crazy. Deep breathing and a mantra or a quick 5-minute meditation on Youtube will do the trick.

## Have Some Sex

No, really… Sexual arousal can help with creativity and flow. I mean, do I have to twist your arm to convince you that you should have sex right now?

## Create an Outline

An outline eliminates the struggle of staring at a blank screen plus gives you an easy starting point. Jot down ideas, facts, and points about what you're writing. If you're writing an email, use one of the templates in the book to write on the page first. Then start writing.

## Record Your Pitch

A lot of non-writers psych themselves out because blank pages are intimidating. A lot of people can blabber on about topics, but when it comes to writing it down, they freeze. An easy way to bypass this is to record your content via video or audio recording and get it transcribed. You can do this with something like Rev.com or Google Docs which has been improving their audio transcription.

## Loop Instrumentals

For me, headphones mean it's work time. Even if I don't play music, it's a sign that I'm working so I don't respond to people who ask me questions even if I can hear them. When you add in looped instrumental music, you get into a rhythm, and it just flows. Some people listen to music with words, but I find this to be incredibly distracting and makes me less productive and the next thing you know, I just wrote rap lyrics on a client's sales page.

## Create a Swipe File

Swipe files are copies of other people's work you use for inspiration and ideas. Let me say that again… inspiration and ideas. NEVER copy someone's work. That's not ok. Swipe files are great for inspiration. I use a google chrome extension called 'Nimbus Screenshot' to capture mine.

## Write Without Editing

Write and don't stop. Misspelled words, punctuation, spacing, bold, caps, etc. … skip it all. When you start adding things like that you cutoff creative juices from flowing which can throw a wrench into your flow. I know writers who turn off grammar correctors and even have apps that disable the backspace so they can only brain dump. Then they'll transfer to other processors and make edits once all their ideas are down.

## Copy Famous Letters By Hand

Not only do you get the benefit of reading the copy, so it sparks ideas, but the physical act of writing it does something in your brain to spark creativity. I hate hand-writing because it takes me so long but this works by subconsciously following the rhythm from top copywriters. It works, No doubt about it. Do yourself a favor and find your way to Neville Medhora's swipe file on the internet. You'll thank me later.

## COPY CLIFF NOTES

Next time you feel stuck and aren't sure what to write:

1) Juggle
2) Exercise
3) Read fiction
4) Brain drugs
5) Write Facts
6) Take a Siesta
7) Have some sex
8) Create an outline
9) Record Your Pitch
10) Loop instrumentals

11) Create A Swipe File

12) Write without editing

13) Copy Famous Letters By Hand

Get instant access to bonus templates,
worksheets, and notes (worth $147) visit
www.WhyDoYouHateMoneyBook.com

# What's A Funnel And Why Do You Need One?

*"Opportunities don't happen. You create them."*
— Chris Grosser

"What are you just standing there for?

Put yourself to use and help me put this bag of rocks in the trunk."

"Bag of rocks?" I said. "What do you think I was born yesterday? That bag of rocks is a freaking 210-pound body wrapped in a tarp and duct tape, Tommy."

"What are you a doctor!? Help me get him into the trunk before Mom wakes up, or she'll throw you in there with him" he replied. "And you're driving."

Tommy hasn't said a word since he stopped barking commands at me over an hour ago. For the last 47 minutes, I've been counting the trees as they pass by as me and Tommy Two-Shoes drive to no-mans land.

And if it weren't for the thunderous roar of the rumble

strips, the soothing voice of the GPS would have put me to sleep a long time ago.

But if I don't have a co-pilot or GPS telling me where to go, I'm doomed. I'll get lost for hours, side-tracked by shiny objects, and maybe (just maybe) I'll eventually find my way... but it's unlikely.

## How A Funnel Works

The GPS which guided me though no-mans land in my fictional mafia story is the same thing a funnel does for your business.

People go in one way, and come out the other, with every step of the way guided and controlled by you to create a specific experience.

These people might have a good sense of direction and can eventually find their way, but you don't want to leave anything to chance.

You start with the desired outcome than an overview of what's going to happen, and they're lead through each step of the way.

Most people won't argue using a GPS when they have no idea where they are or what direction to go but for some reason, they don't treat their business the same.

If you're approaching a four-way intersection, your GPS doesn't leave the four options open and let you choose. It tells you what to do, and if you make the wrong turn, it redirects you back on track.

You need to give your readers the same step-by-step directions.

Guide them through the journey of being interested in what you have to be a happy customer. Never think your reader will figure it out on there own, cross your fingers, and (somehow) hope they become a customer.

I can't tell you how many businesses make this mistake.

Think about how much time, money, energy, and freedom you could save if your marketing was on autopilot and all you had to do was add more people into a kickass funnel?

A properly designed sales funnels works in every niche imaginable. Period. It's your business GPS and your guide to help turn new readers into customers.

## What Is A Sales Funnel

Generally speaking, sales funnels are like websites on steroids.

When a new prospect gives you their email address, they are dropped into your sales funnel. Once this happens, you can now market to them in different ways.

The concept of sales funnels is simple.

Get your reader to their end goal with turning onto 1-way streets or getting into as little accidents as possible. Without one, your potential customers wander around aimlessly looking at all the shiny objects promising the world in 7 days or less.

# What A Sales Funnel Is NOT

To keep you from getting overwhelmed I want to clear up what a sales funnel is NOT…

## 1. A Mystical Magical Maze

A sales funnel does NOT need to include 36 steps of pages, tagging, segmentation, follow-up, automation rules, and complicated processes.

I'm sure you've seen these diagrams floating around the internet that supersede the most recent plans for life on Mars, but that's not what we're talking about here.

In fact, I'd urge you to stay away from complicated funnels because they're harder to track results… and that's what we care about with direct response marketing, remember?

It can be as simple as 2-5 emails after someone claims a free offer to come in for a consultation. Or it can be a simple Facebook post, to a download, to a thank you page with a one-time offer… the possibilities are endless.

## 2. Only Designed To Jam Sleazy Sales Down Someone's Throat

You can already tell, I hate sleazy car salesman approach to selling. It's short-sided, scummy, and no one likes it. It gives me the chills just thinking about it.

I know I HATE being sold to that way, but when someone takes the time to listen, ask me questions, help me out first, I'm going to buy from them 10/10 times.

Sure you can persuade and 'sell' in a funnel, but you can also 'nurture' your readers. Build a close relationship and bond with your reader, so you have rapport, trust, value, and goodwill over time.

This chapter will focus on a stupidly simple funnel and why it's so important to grow your business.

## COPY CLIFF NOTES

Here are a few things a funnel can do for your business:

- Free up more time

- Nurture new leads to sales

- Make money while you sleep

- Create a tight-knit bond with your clients

- Deliver content to solve someone's problem

- Bring more prospective clients into your world

- Increase revenue and take your business to the next level

- Make you the best and most trusted resource in your market

Yea, it's a good thing.

Get instant access to bonus templates, worksheets, and notes (worth $147) visit www.WhyDoYouHateMoneyBook.com

# How The Stupidly-Simple Funnel Works

*"If you don't design your own life plan, chances are you'll fall into someone else's plan. And guess what they have planned for you? Not much."*

— Jim Rohn

In a second, I'm going to layout two easy funnels that I use with clients, and you can use for your business too. But first, I want to cover the basics.

## 1. Put In, Get Out

Think of a sales funnel as a 'repeatable customer generating machine.'

Infotain, influence, persuade, lead someone through an experience you've created, and help them solve their problem.

It's a place for you to add people which will eventually get you customers and increase sales and profits but you have to guide them through the process.

## 2. The Big Pieces

First, you need to drive traffic to your offer — whether it's free or paid.

You can do it many different ways but here are a the few most common: Facebook ads, Google ads, advertorials, social media posts, blog posts, guest blog, podcasts, joint-venture partners, affiliate offers, etc.

Next, you're going to collect their contact information by giving them something which will solve a problem of theirs.

For online businesses, you'll usually collect name and email. For offline offers, you should collect name, email, and phone so you can follow up appropriately. The more contact information you have, the better for follow up but, the more information you ask for the conversion will likely drop.

Once you collect their information on the landing page, they will be brought to the 'Thank You' page either delivering whatever offer you had for them or giving them another.

For help deciding on what to offer, review the chapter 'How To Use Kickass Copywriting To Make Loads Of Cash Without Being Sales.'

## 3. The Magic Is In The Follow-up

Once you've collected their contact information, the fun starts. On average, this is how your customers will break down:

5% will buy within the first 30 days

15% will buy within the first 90 days** (the majority of your customers)

80% will never buy from you

Those numbers aren't meant to discourage you; they're meant to show you that people need time to trust you and make sure you're not another scam artist. Here's why funnels are so important, especially when you follow-up properly with emails, texts, and retargeting ads.

Again, not everyone will buy from you right away (or ever), but when you have sales funnel in place, they can do so, when they are ready. From there, follow-up, build trust, help, and turn some of those interested people into clients.

## 4. Make Your Message Congruent

One of the biggest mistakes is using a false claim or bold-faced lies to get people to give you their contact information.

I've seen this so many times... overhyped claims that have nothing to do with the offer, flat out lies, promises you can't deliver on, tricks, etc.

Not only is this costing you credibility and trust when you do this, but it also costs you dollars in the bank.

This person will rarely buy from you after they feel cheated. On top of this, if you're using paid traffic your inflating your click-through rates which are royally screwing your conversions on the landing page because the headline and ad have nothing to do with what you're offering.

Here's a huge tip: If you're running Facebook ads, use the same or very similar headline on the ad and landing page. When you do this, the message is congruent and recognizable instead of created a disconnect which can cost you a new fan.

## 5. Test The Waters

If you're the type of person that wants everything to be perfect before you put it out into the world, you're going to get eaten alive. One of the most significant advantages you can have over your competition is the ability to fire first and ask questions later. Seriously.

I've had friends or clients reach out to me telling me about this life-changing program they've spend months developing because it's something they thought that people wanted. Then when time comes to sell it, it's a failure.

Hell, it's happened to me plenty of times so don't feel bad if you do this. Months of your life could have been saved by posts on Facebook to your audience and ask them…

"Hey, I've been getting a lot of moms asking me how I lost my baby weight so quickly. I've been thinking about putting together a post-pregnancy training group for new moms to lose their baby weight. Is that something you'd be interested in?"

Crickets? Next!

Gets interested? Cool, build it as you bring them through it.

As you can see, there are plenty of health and fitness professionals who have built very successful careers very different from each other. So you need to look at what works for your personality, and your audience and that starts with getting it out into the universe.

## 6. Stop Waiting. Do It Now!

*I'm not tech savvy.*
*Where do I even start?*
*I don't know what to use.*
*Funnels are too confusing.*
*This stuff is too complicated.*
*How the hell do I build this thing?*

Just like anything, there are loads of ways you can send your emails and build funnels.

I use ConvertKit for my email service provider and building funnels (sales pages, membership sites, webinars, lead generation pages, etc.) I use ClickFunnels.

Do you have to use them? *Yes or else you'll fail.*

Just kidding, you can use whatever you'd like.

I recommend ConvertKit and ClickFunnels, but all providers have their ups and downs so do research, and pick the one you think is best.

Make sure you download your incredible gift by going to the link at the end of the chapter, and I'll walk you through an actual funnel.

The best part is, if you decide you want to switch over to ConvertKit or ClickFunnels using my affiliate link, I'll send you one of my actual funnels for you to use for free. All you have to do is put in your information and start getting leads. Cool, right?

So, instead of building an elaborate funnel and complicated funnel where you are endlessly tinkering with a million different tools, timers, and gadgets… here is the 'The Stupid-Simple Funnel.'

## Breakdown Of The Stupidly-Simple Funnel

Simple, but it works. The better your offer and the more trust and leverage you can build, the more likely that lead will turn into a customer.

- **Ad:** offer something free (lead magnet) or cheap trial offer

- **Landing page:** trade contact information for something valuable to them

- **Thank you page:** deliver the goods and get them to

take action now (call for a bonus offer, one-time special purchase, join your private membership group, etc.)

- **<u>Follow-up:</u>** build trust and add value with an automated email campaign

Here's an example funnel I've had success with:

We ran a Facebook ad, offering a free (or super cheap) 14-day trial voucher for the first 50 people to claim the offer. When they click the ad, they go to a landing page which captures their name, email, and phone number.

Once they enter their information, they're redirected to the 'Thank You' page which offers a free nutrition consultation (something else super valuable), so they take action right away. If they don't take action right away, they're put into an autoresponder sequence with follow-up emails, texts, and retargeting ads.

If you're a chiropractor, you can do the same: Facebook ad for a free or ridiculously cheap consultation, x-rays, etc. The landing page collects their name, email, and phone number. Once they're redirected, give them a reason to call and book right this second — like a free adjustment. Now you have their contact information and can follow up by writing great emails, through text, and with retargeting ads.

## COPY CLIFF NOTES

Stupid-Simple Funnel Checklist

### Referral source:

- Attention-grabbing headline
- Compelling copy
- Offer something that will solve a big problem
- Clear call to action
- Relatable picture (if running an ad)

### Landing page:

- Congruent headline and look
- Give clear instructions on what to do next
- Only one place to go — opt-in
- Call to action
- Keep it clean and simple

### Thank You, page:

- Deliver the goods
- Thank and welcome them
- Clear call to action (call now, one-time purchase, join group, check email, etc.)

## Automated email campaign:

- Confirm email

- Deliver the goods

- Get a response early on

- Thank and welcome them

- Introduce yourself or your company

- Send a series of emails to solve their problem, build trust, show social proof, tell stories, become friends.

Get instant access to bonus templates, worksheets, and notes (worth $147) visit www.WhyDoYouHateMoneyBook.com

# How To Discover The Hidden 'Magic' In Your Funnels

*"I have not failed.*
*I've just found 10,000 ways that won't work."*
— Thomas A. Edison

Once you get your sales funnel up and running, you can test and tweak it find out what converts best.

I recommend only testing one thing at a time like the offer, headline, or hook because then you can see what makes a difference. If you change the entire funnel, then you don't know what caused the increase or increase in conversions.

Once it's optimized, all you have to do is get more people into your funnel.

If you know a certain percentage of people go through your funnel and become customers, you can throw as much money as you want to your funnel with paid traffic because you know your return on investment.

Let that sink in for a minute, and I'll give you an example.

## Gym-Trial Funnel Breakdown

Say you're offering a voucher for a 14-day trial at your gym and are collecting leads for $5 each.

After having a 100 people through your funnel, twenty claimed the coupon because your follow-up and outreach is garbage.

Of those twenty 14-day trails, ten decided to sign up for a package which is $199/month with a 3-month minimum contract ($597.)

Here's the best part... you already know your average customer stays with you for 6-months, so you're looking at $1194.

Let's break that down quick:

    100 x 5 = $500 for 100 leads

    500 / 20 = $25 per 14-day trial lead

    10 x 597 = $5,970 sold after the 14-day trial

    5,970 - 500 = $5,470 revenue after subtracting original ad costs

    1,194 x 10 = $11,940 total based on how long the average client stays

All of those numbers are all on the low-side of what I would expect.

The truth is, you can get leads much cheaper with an irresistible offer, copy, and funnel. You can convert more than leads to trials with a decent follow-up process. You can convert more than 50% of your trials into memberships especially if you're good at sales and have a great product or service (which you better.)

The $11,940 would be 3-5 times more than (minimum) if you do it right. And if you have other offers like nutritional coaching and private 1:1 session that can increase even more.

Are you starting to see the possibilities here?

You can put in $500 into this 'machine' and know you're going to make $5,470 within 14-days and $11,940 over the next six months... what if you put in $2,000?

What if you had a better converting funnel, got cheaper leads, and converted more clients because now you know how to emphasize and sell without selling out?

The possibilities are endless.

## COPY CLIFF NOTES

**Look deeper than what you make on the 'front-end.'**

What if your funnel is a mess, you have no idea how to run ads, and this book didn't help you learn how to write copy?

You spend $300 and only get ONE person to sign up for a 3-month membership at $597, so you make $297 ($597 sale - $300 on ads.)

First, stop what you're doing go to the end of the book where you can learn about hiring me, do this as soon as possible.

Second, look at what happens after. I gave an example before of a customer staying for 6-months so, you will still make $894 profit on that customer.

But what if your average customer stays with you a year because you do such a fantastic job?

This $300 client (I'm still laughing at how high this number is) ends up bringing in a profit of $2,088 ($2,388 a year - $300 spent on ads to bring them in.)

If you're a chiropractor, dentist, physical therapist, etc., a paying client can mean hundreds and even thousands.

Based on the number of people with back-pain how many of them do you think would continue treatment if they came into your chiropractic facility for a free consultation and adjustment and you helped them up front? A ton!

The free offer (or cheap trial) is a low barrier to get them in so you can build trust, rapport, and show them you can help.

Get instant access to bonus templates,
worksheets, and notes (worth $147) visit
www.WhyDoYouHateMoneyBook.com

# The Course Correct
# And Counter Punch

*"So be sure when you step, step with care and great tact.
And remember that life's A Great Balancing Act. And
will you succeed? Yes! You will, indeed (98 and 3/4
percent guaranteed) Kid, you'll move mountains."*

— Dr. Suess

Information is useful, learning is good, listening is smart, but ACTION is excellent.

Put the principles and tactics in this book to work. Try them yourself and learn first hand which work best for your business and which don't (this is critical.)

Action is the best teacher I know which is why I loved boxing so much. It's so closely related to business and life:

You go in with a plan and prepare the best you can, and you know with 100% certainty that once you step inside the ring, it's inevitable you're going to get punched in the face a few times.

You just hope you've prepared enough to shake it off.

Once it happens, it's your turn to land a few clean shots to get your confidence booming. But it doesn't take long before you eat a few more body shots before the first ding of the bell.

In between rounds you get to reflect, rest, and get ready to repeat. But you're more prepared because you know what worked and what didn't work from the last round. You know what course corrections you need to make.

But as the fight continues, the story starts to change. You start feeling worn down, and the seemingly effortless task of breathing becomes difficult.

The next time you get punched in the face, you can feel blood pouring out of your nose. Your eyes water as you taste thick clots of snot and blood drip down the back of your throat making it nearly impossible to breathe.

But there's still a gloved man trying to take your head off with a right hook, and you know you can't stand there and do nothing. Panic sets as your feet drag around the ring and your punches lose steam.

At this point, you have to make a decision. Only this choice you're going to make was decided weeks, months, and years leading up to this moment.

It was decided during your preparation.

All of the coaching, learning, knowledge, networking, systems, experiences, connections, and skills you've created and learned up until this point in time.

*What do you know?*

*Who's in your corner?*

*What do you believe?*

*Why are you doing this?*

*What do you want in life?*

*What mark do you want to leave on this earth?*

*How can you best help the people in your life?*

The fight isn't over, and the best part is, you have no idea what's going on in your opponent's mind.

Sure you might feel shitty, but there's a good chance they feel 10x worse, and the best is yet to come.

You see, you've been paying attention this whole time because you're always learning, growing, and looking for opportunities to win and to get better.

As your opponent lowers his right glove and his eyes fixate on your left ribcage, everything you know to be true tells you a vicious body shot is coming. The hook isn't a setup shot; it's a punch packed with pure evil intentions. This is the type of shot when you can feel your ribs crack as the blow lands.

You have two options based on everything you've learned to this point.

## Option #1: Sit There And Take The Blow

You're too hard headed to learn, adjust, and take action from everything you've learned in the past.

The thing is, this shot won't kill you, it will only break your ribs. You'll likely live to fight another day until one day you completely break by not realizing you're still making the same mistakes.

Option 1, is NOT taking action on what you learned in this book and eventually driving your business directly into the ground or burning out.

Unfortunately, this is the option that most people will take after reading this book.

They'll put it on their bookcase with the other dust collectors gathering information and never apply the right tools they need to build a successful business that makes them happy. Do NOT do this.

## Option #2: Course Correct And CounterPunch

You've already seen what life has thrown your way and you know the consequences if you stay on the same path. But you know there's no sense in sitting there and taking the beating while smacking your head against the wall.

So this time you decide things are going to be different.

You decide to move and move fast. You choose to take action

and turn the reactive state into an attack because now YOU get to determine what's going to happen next.

Course correct and counterpunching is what I want for you, and what I hope this book helps you do.

I wrote this book for a reason:

In a perfect world you're going to use what you learned in this book to help as many damn people as you can, and build a business you love by making a change in this world.

In an imperfect world, this book goes right onto your bookshelf and never gets opened again as you continue to buy every book on Amazon looking for that one unique thing that's going to line it all up for you.

I'd like to leave you with one more piece of truth that I hope you take to heart:

You have the tools to create a business you love; you just need to build momentum.

But it at all starts with one step... then another... and then another.

Over and over again. Because confidence, familiarity, and rhythm make goals that once seemed impossible, just a few giant steps away.

Once you understand this, you have the power to WRITE your way into your wildest dreams.

# Conclusion: Go Kick-Ass

*"I have come here to chew bubblegum and kick ass...*
*and I'm all out of bubblegum."*

— Roddy Piper

Thank you for allowing me to bring you through this new and exciting journey into in the world of copywriting and direct response marketing.

Right now I'm sure you're feeling both excited and overwhelmed.

Rest assured, the strategies and concepts in this book didn't take me a few hours or a couple of dollars to learn. It took years of trial and error, tens of thousands of dollars, sleepless nights of work, countless hours of study, and many failures.

What you'll find in this book is the exact process I use to write high-converting copy for my clients which is why this is extremely valuable to you and the reason I wanted to write this for you.

In a second I'll show you how to fast track your progress even more, but first I want you to realize you have the shortcut I wish I had years ago and is now a future resource for you. Don't just read it and forget about it.

The most important lessons of this book are the templates, ideas, summaries, questions, and notes found in the 'Copy Cliff Notes' section at the end of each chapter.

Not only are the concepts simple to understand, but they can be rapidly applied to any business to start attracting more customers and improving sales right away.

I think you'll surprise yourself how much you can remember when you review these punchy nuggets of copywriting gold which is why I compiled them along with additional bonuses for you grab at no extra charge when you claim your free gift.

If you're wondering where to start, this is what I recommend:

1) Read the book
2) Grab your incredible gift
3) Use the 'Copy Cliff Notes'
4) Practice ***

If you're impatient (like me) and want to fast-track the process, this is where the fun starts.

As helpful as this book will be for you, it's not as beneficial as seeing real-life examples, deep dives into these topics, me walking you through the lessons, and having me there to consult or ask questions, which is why I'm inviting you to join Kickass Copywriting.

www.joeypercia.com/kickasscopywriting

The lessons in this book are a fantastic start, but for more in-depth training and speed-learning to exponentially improve your ability to make money and grow your business, Kickass Copywriting will help you get there faster than ever.

Whether you're a new business owner or season entrepreneur, this will show you the in's and out's of copywriting and marketing including proven copywriting formulas, done-for-you templates, copy critiques and so much more.

Kickass Copywriting is my flagship online copywriting course perfect for people who are not natural born writers (like myself) but want to learn a more natural way to write words that sell without spending 10's of thousands to hire a copywriter.

It's packed with the best kept copywriting secrets from million-dollar marketers so you can sell your ideas, products, and services better than ever.

The best part is when you join you'll get access to everything you need to know about writing words that sell, and can do it from anywhere in the world. All you need is your computer/phone, and an internet connection to watch the lessons and easily apply to your business.

Go to the link below to see if Kickass Copywriting is right for you:

www.joeypercia.com/kickasscopywriting

When you complete the course you'll have all the tools you need to write compelling and infotaining stories, social media posts, Facebook ads, squeeze pages, emails, sales pages, and so much more.

I won't even mention the kick-ass bonuses that come along with the course or the fact that you can try it 100% Risk-Free with my 30-day money back guarantee. If you don't learn anything new and aren't satisfied with the course just ask for your money back within 30-days and it's yours.

I can't promise this special price or the bonuses will last very long, so head over to the page to see if this is the right fit for you.

See you on the inside,

– Joey Percia

# About The Author

*"When the door of opportunity opens, nobody is gonna drag your ass through it."*

— Andy Frisella

Hey, my name is Joey Percia.

I'm a former fitness coach turned copywriter and marketing consultant who helps badass entrepreneurs grow their businesses without selling out.

I'm an average dude born without life-changing talent. Over the years I've failed more times than I can count and suffered from a self-crippling fear surrounding money for most of my life.

I learned a long time ago I learned a valuable lesson… Opportunity presents itself only after you go out and earn it, so that's what I've learned how to do and the skills in this book are tools for me to do that.

Over a decade ago, I started my career as a health and fitness professional. After receiving my graduate degree in Exercise Science, I began traveling, interning, getting certified by, connecting with, and working for top health and fitness industry experts.

Now I write, coach, and consult with these reputable coaches, brands, and companies I've looked up to for years. These industry experts now credit my approach to copywriting and marketing as "genuine, refreshing, and badass."

I've had rockstar clients in many different industries including dating, pharmacy, cannabis, habit-building, digital marketing, online business development, self-development, real estate, chiropractic, and of course other health and fitness related businesses like you'll read about in this book.

When I'm not scouring the earth for the worlds best fish tacos, I speak at seminars and use this book, my course, and my coaching community to show others what I've learned and continue to learn as life throws me it's world-famous curveballs.

To connect with me, join my tribe, and get cool stuff visit www.JoeyPercia.com

# How To Hire Joey

I've had rockstar clients with various businesses in all different industries. Are you interesting in being next?

We can tag-team your copy with copywriting critiques and coaching calls to improve conversions. I can come in and consult on a current campaign or future project to find money-draining leaks.

Maybe you'd like to have me write every word of your copy while you spend time doing things you're best at.

If you'd rather work more closely with me (instead of joining Kickass Copywriting) go to the link below to apply.

www.JoeyPercia.com/apply

As you can imagine spots to work 1:1 with me are limited, so once you apply, someone on my team will contact you to see if you're a good fit.

If you're accepted, I will personally help you tweak, modify, and spice up your copy to improve conversions and build a following or I will write everything for you, without you even lifting a finger.

# "Thank You!"

I appreciate you taking the time out of your day to read this book.

I hope you enjoyed it. To quote Dwayne Johnson, "My philosophy is, it's always very rewarding when you can make an audience laugh. I don't mind making fun of myself. I like self-deprecating comedy. But I'd like you to laugh with me occasionally, too."

So I hope this has served you well.

Don't forget to claim your gift.

I put some of the most important lessons and templates in this book and put them into summaries, worksheets, and notes for you to download for free for being a reader.

All you have to do to claim your bonuses (worth $147) completely free, go to the link.

www.WhyDoYouHateMoneyBook.com

Made in the USA
Monee, IL
31 January 2020